The Novel in Motion

THE NOVEL IN MOTION

An Approach to Modern Fiction

Richard Pearce

OHIO STATE UNIVERSITY PRESS : COLUMBUS

2/1984
gen.l

Copyright © 1983 by the Ohio State University Press

Excerpts from *A Portrait of the Artist as a Young Man,* by James Joyce. Copyright 1916 by B. W. Huebsch. Copyright renewed 1944 by Nora Joyce. Definitive Text Copyright © 1964 by the Estate of James Joyce. Reprinted by permission of Viking Penguin, Inc., the Society of Authors as the literary representative of the Estate of James Joyce, the Executors of the James Joyce Estate, and Jonathan Cape, Ltd.

Excerpts from *Lolita,* by Vladimir Nabokov, are copyright © 1955 by Vladimir Nabokov. All rights reserved. Reprinted by permission of the Putnam Publishing Group and Mrs. Vladimir Nabokov.

Excerpts from *Pale Fire,* by Vladimir Nabokov, are copyright © 1962 by G. P. Putnam's Sons. All rights reserved. Reprinted by permission of the Putnam Publishing Group and Mrs. Vladimir Nabokov.

Excerpts from *98.6,* by Ronald Suckenick, are reprinted by permission of Fiction Collective, Inc.

Chapter 3, "Reeling through Faulkner," appeared under the title "Reeling through Faulkner: Pictures of Motion, Pictures in Motion" in *Modern Fiction Studies,* Vol. 24, No. 4, © 1979 by Purdue Research Foundation, West Lafayette, Indiana 47907. Reprinted by permission.

The portion of Chapter 4, "From Joyce to Beckett: The Tale that Wags the Telling," entitled "Ulysses" was published in an earlier version entitled "Experimentation with the Grotesque: Comic Collisions in the Grotesque World of *Ulysses*" in *Modern Fiction Studies,* Vol. 20, No. 3, © 1974 by Purdue Research Foundation, West Lafayette, Indiana 47907. Reprinted by permission.

The portion of Chapter 4, "From Joyce to Beckett: The Tale That Wags the Telling," entitled "Samuel Beckett's *Watt* and His Trilogy" was published twice in an earlier version under the chapter title: in the *Journal of Beckett Studies,* No. 7 (Spring, 1982), and in *The Seventh of Joyce,* edited by Bernard Benstock, published in 1982 by the Indiana University Press. Reprinted by permission of the *Journal of Beckett Studies,* the Indiana University Press, and the Harvester Press, Ltd., London.

An earlier version of Chapter 5 was published as "Enter the Frame" in the Spring, 1974 (No. 42), issue of *TriQuarterly.*

An earlier version of Chapter 6 was published as "Nabokov's Black (Hole) Humor: *Lolita* and *Pale Fire*" in *Comic Relief: Humor in Contemporary American Literature,* edited by Sarah Blacher Cohen (Urbana, Illinois: University of Illinois Press, 1978). © 1978 by the Board of Trustees of the University of Illinois. Reprinted by permission.

An earlier version of Chapter 7 was published as "Thomas Pynchon & the Novel of Motion: Where're They At, Where're They Going?" in the *Massachusetts Review,* Vol. 21, No. 1 (Spring, 1980), © 1980 The Massachusetts Review, Inc. Reprinted by permission.

(Continued on page vi)

FOR | KARIN
EMILY
—AND JEAN

(Continued from page iv)

An earlier version of Chapter 10 was published as "Bring Back That Line, Bring Back That Time" in the Spring, 1978 (No. 30), issue of *TriQuarterly*.

Library of Congress Cataloging in Publication Data

Pearce, Richard, 1932–
  The novel in motion.

  Includes index.
  1. American fiction—20th century—History and criticism.
2. English fiction—20th century—History and criticism. I.
Title.
PS379.P36 1983   813′.5′09   82-24565
ISBN 0-8142-0345-0

CONTENTS

Introduction: The Novel in Motion   ix

CHAPTER ONE

Toward the Novel in Motion: Movement and the
Narrative Eye   3

CHAPTER TWO

From Realism to Modernism: Two Pictures in
Joyce's *Portrait*   11

CHAPTER THREE

Reeling through Faulkner   24

CHAPTER FOUR

From Joyce to Beckett: The Tale That Wags the Telling   38

CHAPTER FIVE

Enter the Frame: The Loss of Clarity   56

CHAPTER SIX

Dislocation in Nabokov's Black (Hole) Humor:
Lolita and *Pale Fire*   66

CHAPTER SEVEN

Where're They At, Where're They Going?: Thomas Pynchon
and the American Novel in Motion   83

CHAPTER EIGHT

Robert Coover's Kaleidoscopic Spectacle   102

CHAPTER NINE

Riding the Surf: Raymond Federman, Walter Abish,
and Ronald Sukenick   118

CHAPTER TEN

Bring Back That Line, Bring Back That Time   131

Notes   145

Index   153

INTRODUCTION

The Novel in Motion

"We shall sing of the man at the steering wheel." F. T. Marinetti

The dynamo—revolving "at some vertiginous speed" within arm's length of Henry Adams—makes the very earth seem unimpressive "in its old-fashioned, deliberate, annual or daily revolution." And Henry Adams begins to see history as governed by the law of acceleration. Everyone wants to see moving pictures—of people, horses, trains, but especially of the chase in Edwin Porter's *Great Train Robbery* and the "last-minute rescues" of D. W. Griffith. Collision, says Sergei Eisenstein, is the key to montage. Ragtime derives its energy from syncopation—from what were once called "driving notes," or a rhythm that displaces the regular beat and seems to run away from the steady bass. Improvisation, the "break" or "hot lick," is the driving force of jazz. In painting, fixed vantage gives way to shifting perspectives. For Einstein matter is always in motion, and motion determines the size and weight of material objects. Yeats portrays the modern experience in terms of centrifugal force—the falcon "turning in a widening gyre." Leopold Bloom is always on the move, physically and mentally, and the reader of *Ulysses* leaps back and forth between modern and Homeric times. Dos Passos centers on the new automobile, airplane, and movie industries, but, even more, on America's aimless and uncontrollable energy. Hemingway and Fitzgerald picture the ceaseless movement of the Lost Generation. Faulkner's characters run, hunt, gallop, fly, raid, chase, and escape throughout Yoknapatawpha County. The picaro travels through the novel of the fifties. Robbe-Grillet creates a world of shifting landscapes and inscapes. "Where we going?" asks Benny

Profane in Thomas Pynchon's *V*. "The way we're heading," answers Pig Bodine. "Move your ass."

Movement—a creative ideal and a destructive obsession of modern consciousness—dominates the modern novel, especially in America. But what is it that actually moves? Dos Passos relates twentieth-century history to the development of the automobile, the airplane, and the movies. But, except for Charlie Anderson's suicidal race with the speeding train, there is little actual movement in *U.S.A.* Most of the scenes are static, and a thousand pages of pedestrian narrative clog the spirited tempo of the newsreels, biographies, and camera eye. Fitzgerald's characters are restless; and, speeding in Gatsby's yellow roadster, Daisy Buchanan runs over her husband's mistress. But we never see the climactic scene. Among the most memorable images are Daisy and Jordan "buoyed up" on an enormous white couch, the director and his star holding for a kiss beneath the white plum tree, and the enormous eyes of Doctor T. J. Eckleburg staring out from a faded billboard. Hemingway mastered the pure sequence of movement in bullfights and fishing; but there is far more talk than action in *The Sun Also Rises*, and "Big Two-Hearted River" conveys far more inner tension than outward movement.

Movement is the continuous going from point to point, the process of changing places, or displacement. But a writer cannot continually focus on the going or changing without sacrificing a density that traditional readers expect in a novel. Faulkner's *Pylon* contains pages and pages where nothing happens except that the reporter—sometimes alone, sometimes with the flyers whose story he is covering—crosses town from the newspaper office to the hotel to his apartment to the airport, always against the current of the Mardi Gras crowds. This movement dominates the novel after the hero crashes. It is intensified by the descriptions of eating and drinking, and it intensifies the dramatically central descriptions of the air races.[1] But *Pylon* has been one of Faulkner's least-read or -discussed novels because it does not satisfy conventional expectations for characters with deeper motivations or richer complexities. Faulkner could satisfy these expectations in his portrayals of such flat characters as Jason Compson and the Snopeses. And he could evoke the sensation of motion not only by focusing on the continual movement of his characters but through his continual and disorienting shifts of focus—even upon motionless subjects. Indeed, we can distinguish between his pictures *of* motion (where his subjects run, ride, chase, or flee) and his pictures *in* motion (where the narrative eye continually shifts, fragments, and flashes). I hope to show that the sensation of motion is greater when we are directly engaged by the kinetic power of the medium than when we are indirectly engaged by the movement of characters.

First, we must ask how we sense and detect movement—and we should be aware that to sense (or simply feel) and to detect (or find information) are not the same, nor do they necessarily accompany one another. We sense and detect movement when our equilibrium is disturbed and we feel that movement *directly* in our bodies (this is called proprioception). We detect movement but sense it with less intensity when we perceive a displacement outside or at a distance (this is called exteroception). The most sensitive detector of direct movement is the complex system in our inner ear, where specialized organs are designed to move and, therefore, to directly convey each movement of the head: turning, lifting, and lowering movements are conveyed directly by organs that drag and bend tiny hairs. Equally direct is the movement conveyed through changing bone and muscle relations, and through the displacement of stimuli on the skin surface.[2]

Seeing is a more complex process. We see movement at a distance; therefore it is not conveyed directly upon our eyes. Nonetheless, our eyes do move to locate a moving object in the very narrow area of acute vision and to follow its movement. Moreover, our eyes move constantly to scan the field before us and search out structures—even when the field contains no movement at all. Indeed, our eyes move even to scan mental images when dreaming and thinking. It is well known that our eyes move while dreaming. It is less well known that they move when we picture a situation in our minds; but this can be verified easily by asking someone to count the windows in his living room, and watching his eyes move as he counts them.[3] Of course, we are not always conscious of our eye movements. That is, we do not always detect the fact that they move; but we do have kinetic sensations, and the more radical the displacements, the more conscious we are that they are sensations of movement.

Reading a novel is like seeing—experience at a distance that affects us indirectly. It is experience at a distance in three ways. The first is physical: what happens to a character does not happen to us directly. The second is temporal: the story told by the narrator has already happened by the time we encounter his words in the printed text. The third results from the intervention of the

medium: our direct stimuli are words—the product of an inter-
vening narrator, a set of complex signs and symbols, a series of
printed objects—that distance us from what happened in varying
degrees, depending on the convention.

But reading, like seeing, has its own kinetic potential. We can be
made to feel our own dislocations and displacements in the act of
reading. What stimulates these sensations is the very medium
that distances us from narrated events: the intervention of the
narrator as he selects details and frames events; and the intervention of the printed language as it embodies the narrator's voice,
alludes to references beyond the story, and exists as its own
physical presence. Indeed, the medium can stimulate the sensation of motion directly by engaging us in the event of its own
dynamic.

The traditional narrator, who often suppresses the act of narrative intervention, tells us what *happened* and what *was there* by
covertly processing details for us. He selects them for us and
arranges them to advance the story, establish a character, evoke
a mood, focus the symbolism, or geometrically simplify the scene
by moving from left to right, top to bottom, or near to far. But
another mode of narration—established by Smollett and developed by Dickens, Conrad, Joyce, and Faulkner—engages us
directly in the narrator's experience of excited perception. It does
not process details but records the dynamic of the searching eye as
it scans the field to discover what *is happening* and what *is there*.
It causes us to feel the kinetic sensation. Modern novelists also engage us in the events of the dynamic medium and stimulate us
kinetically through dislocations that jolt our mental equilibrium.
We are made to experience shifting points of view, changing
frames of reference, and unpredictable transformations. And
recent novelists have discovered how to stir us physically by
creating syntactical and typographical rhythms that accelerate
the pace of reading.

Paradoxically, attention to seeing did not lead to clearer
pictures on the screen of our visual imagination. More vivid, yes—
but not clearer. Indeed, as we are drawn into the act of excited perception, it becomes more difficult to hold on to an image, let alone
grasp the whole scene. The frame is broken; the picture flies to
pieces. But, then, we do not normally *see* clear pictures. Joel
Snyder traces the popular confusion between the picture and what
we see back to Alberti, who invented the system of perspective
painting. Alberti did not advocate painting what was seen; his

picture was a "rational structure of perceptual judgments." If his kind of picture seems to be validated by the "realistic" photograph, this is because the camera was designed to be an aid to the painter. Lens-makers were instructed by the artists; each new step in the development of the camera was designed to meet the needs of the painter following in Alberti's line.[4] When writers went beyond even what an individual might see to shift perspectives, when they changed the frames of reference, when they brought their very medium into the plane of action, what we see on the screen of our visual imagination becomes even less clear, even more difficult to grasp. The experience may be best described—to use a term from modern physics but equally applicable to all the modern arts—as "unpicturable." As René Guilleré put it fifty years ago in his essay on the jazz age:

> Antique perspective presented us with geometrical concepts of objects—as they could be seen only by an ideal eye. Our perspective shows us objects as we see them with both eyes—gropingly. We no longer construct the visual world with an acute angle, converging on the horizon. We open up this angle, pulling representation against us, upon us, toward us. . . . We take part in this world. That is why we are not afraid to use close-ups in films: to portray a man as he sometimes seems to us, out of natural proportions, suddenly fifty centimeters away from us; we are not afraid to use metaphors, that leap from the lines of a poem, or to allow the piercing sound of a trombone to swoop out of the orchestra, aggressively.[5]

We may distinguish, then, between the novel *of* motion and the novel *in* motion. The novel *of* motion focuses on the movement of its subject; the movement is at a distance and is conveyed to us indirectly. The novel *in* motion may focus on a subject that moves fast or slowly or even stands still, but it engages us directly in the dislocations of the narrative medium. It continually disrupts our equilibrium and imparts the sensation of motion with disturbing immediacy. It draws us into an experience of multiplicity and indeterminacy—or an experience of modern consciousness. It also draws us into an experience of temporality—the dynamic of history. This is a continual joining of the old and the new, the known and the unknown, a movement that seems ungovernable, unpredictable, threatening, but also full of possibility. Without a frame of reference, a stable center, an "objective" point of view, a reliable map or guide, the novel in motion compels us to take full responsibility for our perceptions and judgments.

I have written *The Novel in Motion* for the general scholarly reader as well as the specialist; the later chapters, therefore, are more descriptive and designed for those who may not be familiar with the more contemporary writers. My thesis has developed inductively over the past ten years, through a series of empirical analyses that began during a sabbatical year when I was reading intensely in the history of physics and film, and when I also discovered that the principles of film analysis could illuminate a great deal about what we see in narrative fiction. I would like to express my appreciation to Wheaton College for the grant that helped initiate my project, for the A. Howard Meneely Chair, which gave me time to complete it, and to my colleague Vaino Kola for his drawing of the duck-rabbit. I would also like to thank Caryn James for her resourceful assistance in research and editing and Beverly Clark for her helpful suggestions. I owe a great deal to Raymond Federman for his contagious enthusiasm and critical acumen, to Alan Spiegel for helping me solve some major problems in the development of my thesis, to Melvin Friedman for his continual encouragement and friendship, and to Jean Pearce for her insightful reading, her insistence on clarity, and her responsiveness to a chapter that finally read well.

Early versions of some chapters, before I understood my thesis, and parts of others have been published in various journals and books. I thank the editors for their assistance and permission to republish in this new form: *TriQuarterly*, "Enter the Frame" (Spring 1974) and "Bring Back that Line, Bring Back that Time" (Spring 1978); *Modern Fiction Studies*, "Experimentation with the Grotesque: Comic Collisions in the Grotesque World of *Ulysses*" (Fall 1974) and "Reeling through Faulkner: Pictures of Motion, Pictures in Motion" (Winter 1978–79); *Massachusetts Review*, "Thomas Pynchon and the Novel of Motion in America: Where're They At, Where're They Going?" (Spring 1980); *Comic Relief: Modes of Humor in Contemporary American Literature*, ed. Sarah Blacher Cohen, "Nabokov's Black (Hole) Humor: *Lolita* and *Pale Fire* (University of Illinois Press, 1978); and *The Seventh of Joyce: Selected Papers from the Seventh International James Joyce Symposium*, ed. Bernard Benstock, "From Joyce to Beckett: The Tale That Wags the Telling" (Indiana University Press, 1982).

Wheaton College
Norton, Massachusetts

The Novel in Motion

CHAPTER ONE

Toward the Novel in Motion:
Movement and the Narrative Eye

Daniel Defoe is well known for his realistic detail. But in *Moll Flanders*, he does not give us a single description—only lists of Moll's clothes and statements about her beauty—until a third of the way through the book. And what a scant picture: "One Night I had the Curiosity to disguise my self like a Servant Maid, in a Round Cap and a Straw Hat, and went to the Door."[1] In *Robinson Crusoe* he does not provide a single description of the storm, although "such a dismal sight I never saw."[2] Moreover, the details from which the reader must draw a picture of the island are abstract and quantitative: compass directions, circles, rows, yards.

Samuel Richardson's Pamela is away from home for the first time, discovering a new world, writing home with great frequency, and telling her family everything that happens to her—but we *see* hardly anything. She tells us what she was given by her "kind master," yet we do not *see* what anything looks like when she lists "a suit of my late lady's clothes, and a half a dozen of her shifts, and six fine handkerchiefs, and three of her cambric aprons, and four holland ones."[3] It is only when the "barbarous" Mrs. Jewkes intrudes into her life and upsets her equilibrium—and this is in the thirty-second letter—that we are made to *see*. "Now I will give you a picture of this wretch: She is a broad, squat, pursy, *fat thing*. . . . She has a huge hand, and an arm as thick as my waist. . . . Her nose is flat and crooked, and her brows grow down over her eyes: a dead spiteful, grey, goggling eye, to be sure she has. And her face is flat and broad; and as to colour, looks like as if it had been pickled a month in saltpetre."[4]

We are certainly engaged by the scene, but we see very little when Joseph Andrews enters Lady Booby's room to discover "one of the whitest Necks that ever was seen."[5] Nor does Fielding invite

us to see what is happening in the world of *Tom Jones* until after
an introduction comparing the arts of storytelling and cookery
and using sense experience to engage our intellects rather than
our eyes or taste buds; until after a "short description of Squire
Allworthy," which is not a description but the location of Allworthy on the English map and social system and in the novel's
narrative pattern and moral scale; and until after a narrative account of "an odd accident which befell Mr. Allworthy at his return
home. The decent behavior of Mrs. Deborah Wilkins, with some
proper animadversions on bastards." We are finally given a
chance to see what is happening—or what Mr. Allworthy sees
from the terrace—just before presenting his sister with a little
bastard.

> In the midst of the Grove was a fine Lawn sloping down towards the
> House, near the Summit of which rose a plentiful Spring, gushing out
> of a Rock covered with Firs, and forming a constant Cascade of about
> thirty Foot, not carried down a regular Flight of Steps, but tumbling in
> a natural Fall over the broken and mossy Stones, till it came to the bot-
> tom of the Rock; then running off in a pebly Channel, that with many
> lesser Falls winded along, till it fell into a Lake at the Foot of the Hill,
> about a quarter of a Mile below the House on the South Side, and which
> was seen from every Room in the Front. Out of this Lake, which filled
> the Center of a beautiful Plain, embellished with Groupes of Beeches
> and Elms, and fed with Sheep, issued a River, that for several Miles
> was seen to meander through an amazing Variety of Meadows and
> Woods, till it emptied itself into the Sea, with a large Arm of which,
> and an Island beyond it, the Prospect was closed.
> On the right of this Valley opened another of less Extent, adorned
> with several Villages, and terminated by one of the Towers of an old
> ruined Abbey, grown over with Ivy, and Part of the Front which re-
> mained still entire.
> The left Hand Scene presented the View of a fine Park, composed of
> very unequal Ground, and agreeably varied with all the Diversity that
> Hills, Lawns, Wood, and Water, laid out with admirable Taste, but ow-
> ing less to Art than to Nature, could give. Beyond this the country
> gradually rose into a Ridge of wild Mountains, the Tops of which were
> above the Clouds.[6]

But Fielding has allowed us to see the world of *Tom Jones* at the
expense of his story. And he ends his plentiful description with a
warning: "Reader, take care, I have unadvisedly led thee to the
Top of as high a Hill as Mr. *Allworthy's*, and how to get thee down
without breaking thy Neck I do not well know. However, let us e'en
venture to slide down together, for Miss *Bridget* rings her Bell,
and Mr. *Allworthy* is summoned to Breakfast, where I must attend, and, if you please, shall be glad of your Company"
(43–44).

Laurence Sterne is noted for his playful disruptions of the story line, but the first time he invites us to *see* what is happening in the world of *Tristram Shandy* is in the tenth chapter. The first picture is of a saddle owned by the husband of the midwife who brought Tristram into the world. The narrative eye moves from top to bottom of a "demi-peak'd saddle, quilted on the seat with green plush, garnished with a noble row of silver-headed studs, and a noble pair of shining brass stirrups, with a housing altogether suitable, of grey superfine cloth, with an edging of black lace, terminating in a deep, black silk fringe, *poudré d'or*."[7] But this was not the saddle upon which the parson rode, for he fitted his "lean, sorry, jackass of a horse" with such a saddle "as the figure and value of such a steed might well and truly deserve." He left his splendid saddle—the first fully seen element in the novel—hung up behind the study door.

Defoe does not picture Moll Flanders, the storm that threatens Robinson Crusoe, or the island he meticulously cultivates; he lists and counts and forms general outlines. In *Pamela* the epistler does not pause in her account of what happened to show us what anything looks like until the thirty-second letter. In *Tom Jones* "the reader's neck [is] brought into danger by a description." In *Tristram Shandy* the first item described is immediately withdrawn from the narrative; indeed, the playful narrator teases our appetite to see by substituting a picture of what is not *there* in the story for what is *there* but is never seen by the reader. What we discover in the early English novel is a powerful allegiance to the movement of the story, or to the art and joy of storytelling, and a wary regard for the power of seeing. When we are made to see, the narrator is in a singular state of agitation, loses control of the story, or self-consciously toys with our desire for immediacy.

Of course, we visualize in a general way even when the narrator provides few cues. We project our own images, or fill in what Roman Ingarden calls "spots of indeterminacy" even when Pamela lists her gifts.[8] But we do not begin to see until the narrative eye begins to move. In Fielding's description of the view from Allworthy's terrace, the narrative eye moves from near to far and then left to right. In Sterne's picture of the parson's saddle, it moves from top to bottom. What distinguishes Pamela's picture of Mrs. Jewkes is a movement of the narrative eye that is like the movement of our eyes in the act of seeing, and that the moving picture camera accentuates when it pans, tilts, zooms, and shifts from angle to angle. When Pamela, still in a state of heightened agitation, relives the moment she encountered Mrs. Jewkes, she engages us to see not only *what* but *how* she saw. First she takes in the "broad, squat, pursy" figure. Then she focuses on the huge hand, the arm as thick as her waist, the crooked nose, the hanging brows, the goggling eye. And finally she widens her glance (though not as wide as it was at first) to take in the flat, broad, pickled face.

Whether we are agitated or composed, seeing is a form of action. Our eyes are in continual motion, restlessly searching, actively selecting. They scan the field before us, even to see internal images of dreams and thought. They shift five times a second to refocus the spot of sharp vision. As Rudolph Arnheim says, "through the world roams the glance, directed by attention, focusing the narrow range of sharpest vision now on this, now on that spot, following the flight of a distant sea gull, scanning a tree to explore its shape. This eminently active performance is what is truly meant by visual perception."[9]

The first English novel that continually engages us in the act of seeing is Smollett's *Expedition of Humphry Clinker*. Although there may be more physical action in *Joseph Andrews* or *Tom Jones*—the journeys being faster paced and filled with more chasing, escaping, and slapstick—Smollett's reader experiences more activity, or livelier sensations of motion. This is due to the rapid flashes of visual detail and rapid movement of perspective as Matthew, Lydia, Jeremy, Tabitha, and Win report to their different correspondents. Although Matthew orders his perceptions numerically, there is no logic to their sequence. Matthew's eye leaps from one vulgar object to another in the Vauxhall garden, and the reader's eye leaps not only with Matthew's but, through his metaphors and similes, along an even wider range: "Here a wooden lion, there a stone statue; in one place, a range of things like coffee-house boxes, covered a-top; in another, a parcel of alehouse benches; in a third, a puppet-shew representation of a tin cascade; in a fourth, a gloomy cave of a circular form, like a sepulchral vault half-lighted; in a fifth, a scanty slip of grass-plat, that would not afford pasture sufficient for an ass's colt." Then, four pages later, Lydia is "dazzled and confounded with the variety of beauties that rushed all at once upon my eye." Now Vauxhall is

a spacious garden, part laid out in delightful walks, bounded with high hedges and trees, and paved with gravel; part exhibiting a wonderful assemblage of the most picturesque and striking objects, pavilions, lodges, groves, grottoes, lawns, temples, and cascades; porticoes, colonades, and rotundos; adorned with pillars, statues, and painting; the whole illuminated with an infinite number of lamps, disposed in different figures of suns, stars, and constellations; the place crowded with the gayest company, ranging through those blissful shades, or supping in different lodges on cold collations, enlivened with mirth, freedom, and good humour, and animated by an excellent band of musik.[10]

Matthew and Lydia do far more than describe a vista, like the narrator of *Tom Jones*, or list the items of interest, like Robinson Crusoe and Pamela. They convey what Lydia calls the "rush" of objects on their eyes, or, more precisely, the flashing movement of excited perception. And to this movement is added the shifting of perspectives as we leap from one correspondent's vantage to another. Defoe, Richardson, Fielding, and Sterne focus on the movement of their characters—their movement from place to place and their changes in situation. When this kind of movement comes to dominate a novel, it is a novel *of* motion. Although we experience this motion vicariously, it comes to us indirectly, for we are distanced from it by the narrative medium. Smollett engages us in the movement of the narrative eye, to which he adds a shifting of perspectives. That is, he locates the source of movement in the narrative medium—our most immediate point of contact— and, therefore, we experience the sensation of motion directly in the act of reading. Smollett looks forward to the novel *in* motion.

When the novel in motion fully emerges, the medium will not only engage us directly, its energy will become dominant and even autonomous, continually upsetting our equilibrium and ultimately threatening us with a loss of control. Charles Dickens takes us a step closer. Influenced by Smollett, Dickens created novels that are alive with visual vitality—where the narrative eye generates dramatic excitement by flashing from point to point and shifting perspectives by "cutting in" for a close-up and "intercutting" between story lines. Indeed, it creates distortions, animates objects, mechanizes people, develops surprising connections and disconnections so that his world seems to be governed by a life force of its own. Ultimately, Dickens maintains control of this world; as Robert Alter points out, his imagination comes to possess and subdue the alien realm.[11] But the movement of his narrative eye becomes a powerful dramatic force. It is just this movement that influenced D. W. Griffith and Sergei Eisenstein, who realized the potential of the camera—the narrative eye of moving pictures—to generate drama through its own kinds of motion. But Griffith and Eisenstein developed in different ways, and a comparison may help us understand the kind of motion that was generated in the modern novel.

In 1908, while planning a film called *After Many Years*, Griffith proposed that the scene showing Annie Lee waiting for her husband be followed by one showing him cast away on a desert island. But, his employers objected, "how can you tell a story jumping about like that? The people won't know what it's about." Griffith replied, "Doesn't Dickens write that way?"[12] In conceiving *After Many Years*, Griffith was discovering that the narrative eye need not hold still until a scene was played through, that indeed it gained interest as it was broken into a sequence of shots that disrupted the story line, and that it gained vitality as the movement of the camera disrupted the viewer's equilibrium.

This point becomes clear when we measure Griffith's accomplishment against that of Edwin Porter, who created the first notable chase scene in *The Great Train Robbery* (1903). Porter initiated the dynamics of the chase when he cut from the escaping bandits back to the train station and the formation of the posse that would pursue them.[13] But, despite his enormous success, his chase turns out to be one of the slowest in the history of film.[14] We can see why when we turn, first, to Griffith's *Lonely Villa* (1909) and, then, to *The Lonedale Operator* (1911).

Porter cut back in time to show the formation of the posse, but in the actual chase the posse followed the bandits past the camera—which sat still on its tripod by the roadside. In *The Lonely Villa* Griffith cut back and forth between the besieged wife and the husband frantically driving home—decreasing the duration of each shot, and thereby increasing the speed of the action—but the cutting is minimal and the composition is static. *The Lonedale Operator* has far more vitality due to the increased number of cuts and the different kinds of shots. The camera seems in continual motion—focusing now on the telegraph office where Blanche Sweet is trying to protect herself, now outside the building or outside the door where the bandits are trying to break in, now on the train speeding to the rescue, now a full shot, now a close-up, now from one angle, now from another. In each of these films, then, the spectator's experience is progressively intensified by the increased movement of the narrative eye. More and more we feel the displacement; more and more our equilibrium is upset; more and more the motion of the narrative eye intensifies the experience of the chase.

Griffith established the dynamics of the chase—film's "great element of dramatic narraturgy"[15]—because he understood the difference between pictures *of* motion and pictures *in* motion—or the power of the moving camera. Indeed, he continually engaged the spectator in this movement even in scenes of less physical action, by cutting between long establishment shots, medium shots, and close-ups. When he acknowledges his kinship with Dickens, he leads us to see that fiction like film is composed of narrative-pictorial units, and that it too gains a singular vitality when the narrative eye shifts between them.

Actually, it is Eisenstein who led us to understand this in his essay on "Dickens, Griffith, and the Film Today," where he turned a sequence of *Oliver Twist* into a shot-by-shot scenario. He demonstrated how the tension was heightened when the narrative eye cut back and forth between Oliver's capture and the old man waiting with his watch, and his analyses of Dickens revealed a great many other effects achieved through the cutting and joining of disparate shots.[16] Besides Dickens and Griffith, Eisenstein was in fluenced by Dziga Vertov, whose editing was designed to bring workers and machines to life and awaken the spectator to new understanding rather than engage him in the story. He was also attracted by the "jump cuts" in Kabuki drama and the dazzling vitality of Abel Gance, especially as he cut across three screens in *Napoleon*. What Eisenstein emphasized in his cutting was not the development of a story or the joining of story lines but fragmentation, leaping, conflict, and collision—or a movement that continually disrupts the viewer's equilibrium. Although there is very little movement of the camera within the shot, an enormous amount of movement is generated by the rapid cutting between shots as the narrative eye changes its location, distance, and angle and creates its own dynamic rhythm by varying the duration of each take.

Griffith established the dynamics of the chase but kept it within the limits of the story frame. That is, the movement of the camera simply reinforces the movement of the chase; each perspective is clearly grounded, and at the end all the lines are drawn together. Eisenstein destroyed the spatial and temporal limits of the story frame to engage us in the terror or beauty of the motion itself. He engages us in the anxiety of the citizens fleeing down the Odessa steps by radically shifting perspectives, by shooting from points that destroy our sense of space, by fragmenting images, by repeating shots over and over, by drawing out moments to what seem interminable lengths. He can also engage us in the motion of an urban scene to show how his movement is grounded in contemporary reality.

> All sense of perspective and of realistic depth is washed away by a nocturnal sea of electric advertising. Far and near, small (in the *foreground*) and large (in the *background*), soaring aloft and dying away, racing and circling, bursting and vanishing—these lights tend to abolish all sense of real space, finally melting into a single plane of colored light points and neon lines moving over a surface of black velvet sky. . . .
>
> Headlights on speeding cars, highlights on receding rails, shimmering reflections on the wet pavements—all mirrored in puddles that destroy our sense of direction (which is top? which is bottom?), supplementing the mirage above with a mirage beneath us, and rushing between these two worlds of electric signs, we see them no longer on a single plane, but as a system of theater wings, suspended in the air, through which the night flood of traffic lights is streaming.[17]

Eisenstein, then, was following more in the line of Smollett and Dickens than was Griffith, for in liberating his narrative eye from the bounds of realistic perspective, he was giving it an independent life of its own. Indeed, he was extending this line in ways very much like those of Joyce and Faulkner, whom he at least indirectly influenced.

CHAPTER TWO

From Realism to Modernism:
Two Pictures in Joyce's *Portrait*

FLAUBERT, ZOLA, CONRAD

Dickens created a world alive with visual vitality. Flaubert achieved a new level of visual precision, showing us far more than telling us what happened, and even cutting back and forth between actions occurring at the same time. But he does not engage us fully in the dynamic of seeing. Watch how he introduces Emma into the world of Charles Bovary:

> A young woman wearing a blue merino dress with three flounces came to the threshold of the door to receive Monsieur Bovary; she led him to the kitchen where a large fire was blazing. The servants' breakfast was boiling beside it in small pots of all sizes. Some damp clothes were drying inside the chimney-corner. The shovel, tongs, and the nozzle of the bellows, all of colossal size, shone like polished steel, while along the walls hung many pots and pans in which the clear flame of the hearth, mingling with the first rays of the sun coming in through the window, was mirrored fitfully.[1]

In his study of *Fiction and the Camera Eye,* Alan Spiegel points out an important difference between Flaubert and his predecessors. The earlier novelist perceived what was universal and essential about his characters; the senses revealed only what was accidental, secondary, and continually changing. But Flaubert had to *see* his characters—he had to picture them as inseparable from the time and space through which they moved. Emma Bovary is "one in an almost endless series of modern characters who are seen before they are named, who appear first as this man or that woman and only later as Dick Diver or Horace Benbow or Molly Bloom." Indeed, it is not until two paragraphs after her introduction that we realize "that this 'young woman,' whose emergence has been so casual and oblique, is, in fact, 'Mademoiselle Emma,' the same Emma whose name appears in the title of the novel."[2]

But Flaubert has achieved another effect, which will become more clear if we look ahead to Zola. *L'Assommoir* begins with a picture. We see Gervaise at the open window. We see that Gervaise has seen through the window. We see her fling herself across the bed. We see her sitting up. And then we see what she sees from the bed:

> She sat unmoving on the edge of the bed under the faded chintz canopy that hung down to the headboard from a string fastened to the ceiling. Her tear-blurred eyes wandered slowly over the wretched furnished room—a walnut bureau with one drawer missing, three cane-bottom chairs, a small grease-stained table on which stood a battered water jug. For the children's use they had crowded in an iron-frame cot that blocked off the bureau and filled up two-thirds of the floor space. In one corner their trunk gaped open and empty, except for a pile of soiled socks and shirts, with a worn-out man's hat shoved underneath. Along the walls and on chair backs hung a ragged shawl, a mud-crusted pair of trousers, odds and ends of old clothes that even old-clothes dealers would spurn. In the middle of the mantlepiece, between two mismated zinc candlesticks, was a bundle of pawn tickets, pink in color. Yet theirs was the best room in the building, on the second floor facing the street.
>
> The two children were still sound asleep, with both their heads on the same pillow.[3]

It is important to note that we see Gervaise's room not through her eyes but from her position. That is, the narrator, though sympathetic with Gervaise and drawing very close to her, does not select the items in the room to reflect Gervaise's perception—any more than Fielding, who described the vista from Allworthy's terrace but not through his eyes. Fielding and Zola, and Sterne as well, pictured their subjects in a manner that would seem most objective: ordered geometrically from side to side or top to bottom. Zola increased the objectivity by minimizing the presence of his narrator. The result is like a moving picture, where the camera establishes Gervaise's position and emotional state, and then pans each object in the room from her position.

Let me transcribe Zola's passage into a film scenario to make this point more graphic—as well as to focus the narrative-pictorial elements, the moving pattern, and the dramatic effect:

1. Establishment shot of Gervaise sitting on the edge of a bed under a faded chintz canopy. *Cut to*:
2. Close-up of her tear-blurred eyes. *Cut to*:

3. Narrative eye *panning* a walnut bureau with a missing drawer, three cane-bottomed chairs, a small grease-stained table holding a battered water jug, a large iron-frame cot, an empty trunk beside a pile of soiled socks, shirts, and worn-out man's hat, a mantelpiece with two mismated zinc candlesticks and, between them, a bundle of pink pawn tickets. *Hold*:

4. Then *pan* to two children sleeping on the iron cot, their heads on the same pillow.

I have transcribed the scene's major pictorial unit, after the establishment of Gervaise's location and emotional state, as a pan shot—the regular, horizontal turning of the camera or narrative eye. My choice follows Zola's cue: "Her tear-blurred eyes wandered slowly over the wretched furnished room"; but it also derives from Zola's basic regularity—of direction, pace, and attention.

With minor variance due to the conventions of syntax and grammar, Zola's entire scene is governed by the regular movement of the narrative eye. This movement becomes a dramatic force—all the more dramatic and all the more forceful as the narrator's voice becomes less personal and his presence is effectively denied. The narrative eye focuses with even attention, in a steady direction, and with a regular pace: on Gervaise sitting on the bed, on her tear-blurred eyes, on each of the many items of the room, and on the two children sleeping with their heads on the same pillow. As a result Gervaise and the children are rendered very much like objects or things in the room. To see people as objects or things is the tacit goal of objectification—and of realism, which derives from the Latin *res*, or "thing." The source of this objectification in Zola's novel is the leveling movement of the narrative eye.

L'Assommoir is about the leveling of characters; its plot follows the inexorable movement of Gervaise from a lively woman to a witless alcoholic and finally a "bad smell in the corridor," a corpse "in her cubbyhold already turning green." We are made to feel the leveling power through the regular movement of the narrative eye. When we look back at *Madame Bovary*, we recall that Emma too was introduced as an object among objects. When we re-examine her introductory picture, we will discover that it too is formed by a panning of the narrative eye. We may also feel its leveling power and understand that it derives as much from the movement of the medium as from the movement of the story. Even the crosscutting movement of Flaubert's famous county fair scene has the power of leveling, as the narrative eye shifts back and forth between Rodolphe, who is courting Emma, and the official who is announcing the prize for farming and the price of manure.

Reality for the "realist" like Flaubert and Zola can be known only through the senses; therefore the picture becomes more central to his story. The narrative eye begins to compete with the narrative voice. The reader is converted from an auditor to a witness, and we are engaged by the movement of the narrative eye as it becomes a dramatic force in the novel. But although the narrative picture brings us closer to the novel's present and adds to the story's immediacy, we still remain at a remove from what happens—which is one measure of nineteenth-century scientific objectivity. The narrator, though minimizing his presence, nonetheless intrudes into the scene, processes details for us, turns from one to another with mechanical regularity, thereby reducing them to the same level, and arranges them for us geometrically to insure "objective" clarity. That is, he composes, or rearranges, what he has seen.

The more the narrative eye moves, the more we see in a novel—and the more immediate our experience. But the immediacy of our experience depends on the quality even more than the quantity of movement. We do not experience as intense an immediacy in Flaubert and Zola as we do in Smollett and Dickens because the narrative eye moves with such regularity—or, more important, because it is governed by a force other than that of excited perception. The traditional movement of the narrative eye is governed by an a priori purpose and order. Details are selected to advance the action, establish a character, create a mood, focus the symbolism, or, as in Flaubert and Zola, to unobtrusively guide our attention by moving with mechanical regularity. In some sense, of course, every detail will contribute to the narrative and will symbolize or convey more than the fact of its own existence. When details are not patterned to convey a purpose or to organize a scene, they appear random. When the narrative eye leaps from point to point erratically, it destroys our equilibrium and creates a sense of disorder: Matthew Bramble compares Vauxhall to the "precincts of Bedlam," and we come to experience the bedlam of Dickens's London. And when the narrative eye jumps erratically from feature to feature, fragmenting the whole and magnifying the parts, we see a character as grotesque. Pamela's picture of Mrs. Jewkes foreshadows Pip's nightmare encounter with Miss Havisham.

Scenes of bedlam and encounters with the grotesque, though, are only extreme possibilities. More important, the apparently random selection of detail conveys the "rush" of objects on our eyes—or the movement of the eyes as they leap from point to point because their equilibrium has been upset, because they have been aroused and are looking. As E. H. Gombrich points out, "We look when our attention is aroused by some disequilibrium, a difference between our expectation and the incoming message."[4] Studies in eye movement show that fixations are not regular and are concentrated on unpredictable or unusual details.[5] In contrast to traditional picturing, what we might call phenomenal picturing engages us in the act of seeing. In contrast to details selected for some ulterior narrative purpose are details that arouse and attract the narrative eye by their own intrinsic power and interest. In contrast to the regular movement of the narrative eye is a movement aroused by disequilibrium, impelled toward the unexpected.

Joseph Conrad, who pledged himself to the task of making us *see* in *The Nigger of the Narcissus*, extends the line running from Smollett through Dickens. The novel opens, not with a traditional setting of the scene, but with the narrative eye flashing from one part of the ship to another, now focusing on the patterns of light, now stopping to focus an image by way of a simile, now cutting in to a close-up of parts of dress and body. Let me emphasize the details that draw the narrative eye:

> The *main deck was dark* aft, but halfway from forward, *through the open doors of the forecastle, two streaks of brilliant light cut the shadow.* . . . A hum of voices was heard there, while port and starboard, *in the illuminated doorways, silhouettes of moving men appeared* for a moment, very black, without relief, *like figures cut out of sheet tin.* The ship was ready for sea. The *carpenter* had driven in the last *wedge of the main-hatch battens,* and, *throwing down his maul,* had *wiped his face with great deliberation,* just on the stroke of five. The *decks* had been swept, the *windlass oiled* . . . the *big tow-rope lay in long bights* along one side of the main deck, with one *end carried up and hung over the bows,* in readiness for the *tug that would come paddling* and hissing noisily, hot and *smoky,* in the *limpid, cool quietness of the early morning.* . . . The *two forecastle lamps were turned up high,* and shed an intense hard glare; shore-going *round hats were pushed far on the backs of heads,* or *rolled about on the deck* amongst the *chain-cables; white collars, undone, stuck out on each side of red faces; big arms in white sleeves gesticulated.*[6]

Now let me transcribe the last section of Conrad's narrative picture into a shot-by-shot scenario, as Eisenstein did to *Oliver Twist*, to emphasize the movement of the narrative eye as it fragments the scene and continually disrupts our equilibrium:

1. Long shot of two forecastle lamps turned up high, shedding an intense hard glare. *Cut to*:
2. Extreme close-up of shore-going round hats pushed far on the backs of heads. *Cut to*:
3. Hand-held traveling shot of hats rolling about on the deck among the chain-cables. *Cut to*:
4. Extreme close-up of white collars, undone, sticking out on each side of red faces. *Cut to*:
5. Extreme close-up of big arms in white sleeves gesticulating.

TWO PICTURES IN JOYCE'S *PORTRAIT*

Conrad does not process the details of his narrative picture for us. He makes us see the scene as if we were there, our eyes being drawn from one point to another as our attention is aroused by some new disequilibrium. But the narrative eye still does not function dramatically. The first novel to make dramatic use of such eye movement is James Joyce's *A Portrait of the Artist as a Young Man*, for it focuses on the development of a writer's perception. It is especially interesting because it bridges traditional and phenomenal picturing, and even takes a step toward what might be called modernist picturing. When young Stephen Dedalus is caught in "the whirl of a scrimmage," he bends over to look through his legs. "The fellows were struggling and groaning and their legs were rubbing and kicking and stamping. Then Jack Lawton's yellow boots dodged out the ball and all the other boots and legs ran after."[7] His equilibrium is destroyed. Literally upside down, Stephen's view is captured for us phenomenally. But this is one of the exceptions in the major part of the novel. The others, which are less visual than dramatic, are the three epiphanies ending with Stephen and E— C— waiting for the last tram—and these he "chronicled" after his move to Dublin, which mentally destroyed his equilibrium, "reshaping the world about him" (67).

In the first four chapters, Joyce conveys Stephen's responses as an infant, a young child, an adolescent, and a young man with great skill and immediacy. He renders the stream of consciousness with new plausibility, but his pictures—what Stephen sees —are traditional. With the exception of Father Arnall's sermon (where the images are powered by rhetoric) and Stephen's idealized vision of the wading girl, the pictures are not vivid. Surprisingly, in the fifth chapter, just when Stephen is most introspective and cerebral, the pictures take on a new quality and his visual experience becomes most intense and kinetic. Stephen does not picture the backside of Venus Praxiteles, where Lynch inscribed his name, or see the basket carried by the butcher boy; he uses them to illustrate his aesthetic theory. Nor is he disturbed by the "long dray laden with old iron" that covers the end of his discourse "with the harsh roar of jangled and rattling metal" (209). Yet this chapter contains the greatest quantity of visual details, which are seen most sharply, often for what seems to be their own intrinsic interest rather than some narrative purpose. And the movement of the narrative eye from point to point within the scene and within Stephen's consciousness is faster and less regular.[8] Compare, for instance, two passages that focus on Stephen drinking tea—one from the early pages of the novel, when Stephen's senses are most acute, the other from the opening of chapter five, right after he has not seen but transformed a wading girl into a "strange and beautiful seabird" or "wild angel . . . an envoy from the fair courts of life" (171,172).

A

The bell rang and then the classes began to file out of the rooms and along the corridors towards the refectory. He sat looking at the two prints of butter on his plate but could not eat the damp bread. The tablecloth was damp and limp. But he drank off the hot weak tea which the clumsy scullion, girt with a white apron, poured into his cup. He wondered whether the scullion's apron was damp too or whether all white things were cold and damp. Nasty Roche and Saurin drank cocoa that their people sent them in tins. They said they could not drink the tea; that it was hogwash. Their fathers were magistrates, the fellows said. (12–13)

B

He drained his third cup of watery tea to the dregs and set to chewing the crusts of fried bread that were scattered near him, staring into the dark pool of the jar. The yellow dripping had been scooped out like a boghole and the pool under it brought back to his memory the dark turfcoloured water of the bath in Clongowes. The box of pawn-tickets at his elbow had just been rifled and he took up idly one after another in his greasy fingers the blue and white dockets, scrawled and sanded and creased and bearing the name of the pledger as Daly or MacEvoy.

1 Pair Buskins.

1 D. Coat.

3 Articles and White.

1 Man's Pants.

Then he put them aside and gazed thoughtfully at the lid of the box, speckled with lousemarks, and asked vaguely:

—How much is the clock fast now?

His mother straightened the battered alarmclock that was lying on its side in the middle of the kitchen mantlepiece until its dial showed a quarter to twelve and then laid it once more on its side. (174)

Obviously passage B is longer than passage A, but this does not invalidate the comparison. Quite the contrary, for if we search back through the first four chapters of *Portrait*, we will find no descriptive passage (except for Father Arnall's rhetorical description of Hell) as long as the passage that opens chapter five. There is more description in chapter five, and each picture contains a greater quantity of detail. There is also a qualitative difference. We see far more when Stephen "drained his third cup of watery tea to the dregs" than when he "drank off the hot weak tea." We are engaged in the act of seeing when the narrative eye focuses first on his "chewing the crusts of fried bread that were scattered near him" and then on his "staring into the dark pool of the jar." Moreover, the narrative eye shifts from physical to mental images, from the "pool" of "yellow dripping" to the "turfcoloured water of the bath in Clongowes." Then it shifts to the pawn tickets—to each separate ticket—then to the box lid "speckled with lousemarks," then to his mother straightening the alarm clock, showing its face, and laying it back on its side.

Of course, we find some sharp images in the first four chapters. We will also find many general and idealized images in the fifth, for Stephen remains an aesthetician and a self-conscious creator even while developing his new visual capacities. But these passages are exemplary. With the opening of the last chapter, there is a dramatic increase in the number of visual details. They are grasped more sharply by the narrative eye, which reflects Stephen's consciousness. They often appear irrelevant to what is happening in the narrative or to what Stephen is saying or thinking; and if they are not irrelevant, they are, in comparison with the earlier section, excessive or gratuitous—seen, that is, for their own intrinsic attraction.[9] And the narrative eye moves with palpable swiftness from one to the other, often fragmenting the scene, the action, or the subject being pictured.

Even when Stephen is most introspective and abstract, he passes a man, for the first time, near the canal: "the consumptive man with the doll's face and the brimless hat coming towards him down the slope of the bridge with little steps, tightly buttoned into his chocolate overcoat, and holding his furled umbrella a span or two from him like a diviningrod" (177). He recollects Cranly, wondering why he could never raise before his mind the entire image of his body but only the image of the head and face? Even now against the grey curtain of the morning he saw it before him like the phantom of a dream, the face of a severed head or deathmask, crowned on the brows by its stiff black upright hair as by an iron crown. It was a priestlike face, priestlike in its pallor, in the widewinged nose, in the shadowings below the eyes and along the jaws, priestlike in the lips that were long and bloodless and faintly smiling. (178)

Later, after the long and conventional description of the dean of studies lighting a fire and comparison of the priest's face to an "unlit lamp or a reflector hung in a false focus" (187), Stephen mentally recomposes the "forms of the community" from the "gustblown vestments" with a fragmentary swiftness that approaches the narrative pictures in "Circe":

the dean of studies, the portly florid bursar with his cap of grey hair, the president, the little priest with feathery hair who wrote devout verses, the squat peasant form of the professor of economics, the tall form of the young professor of mental science discussing on the landing a case of conscience with his class like a giraffe cropping high leafage among a herd of antelopes, the grave troubled prefect of the sodality, the plump roundheaded professor of Italian with his rogue's eyes. They came ambling and stumbling, tumbling and capering, kilting their gowns for leap frog, holding one another back, shaken with deep fast laughter, smacking one another behind and laughing at their rude malice, calling to one another by familiar nicknames, protesting with sudden dignity at some rough usage, whispering two and two behind their hands. (192)

He glimpses a fellow student's "wheypale face," its "oblong skull . . . overgrown with tangled twinecoloured hair" (193) and Cranly's dark eyes watching him "from under the wide falling leaf of a soft hat" (194). There is a flash of MacCann, with a "silverwrapped tablet of mild chocolate which peeped out of [his] breastpocket," who smiles broadly and tugs twice "at the strawcoloured goatee which hung from his blunt chin" (196). Again the dean of studies is caught by the flashing narrative eye, "his threadbare soutane gathered about him for the ascent with womanish care. . . . As he spoke he wrinkled a little his freckled brow and bit, between his phrases, at a tiny bone pencil" (199). Then, during Stephen's aesthetic discourse, he catches Lynch rubbing "both his hands over his groins but without taking them from his pockets"; "his long slender flattened skull beneath the long pointed cap brought before Stephen's mind the image of a hooded reptile" (205). And a few moments later the discussion is interrupted by a "fat young man wearing a silk neckcloth. . . . His pallid bloated face expressed benevolent malice and, as he had advanced through his tidings of success, his small fatencircled eyes vanished out of sight and his weak wheezing voice out of hearing" (210).

At the end of the aesthetic discourse and their walk, Stephen and Lynch come upon E— C—, preparing to go off with her companions. In a singular picture the narrative eye captures Stephen's view of the scene; this is all we see:

> The quick light shower had drawn off, tarrying in clusters of diamonds among the shrubs of the quadrangle where an exhalation was breathed forth by the blackened earth. Their trim boots prattled as they stood on the steps of the colonnade, talking quietly and gaily, glancing at the clouds, holding their umbrellas at cunning angles against the few last raindrops, closing them again, holding their skirts demurely. (216)

This narrative picture is singular because we do not see E— C—, whom in the next paragraph Stephen compares to a simple, strange, and willful bird; and who, on the next page, inspires Stephen—his limbs bathed in "pale cool waves of light," "his soul . . . all dewy wet"—to compose his villanelle (217). It is singular, that is, because of its contrast to the abstract, vague, or idealized pictures that dominate Stephen's imagination, and because it contrasts with the narrative pictures that dominate the first four chapters. Recall the scene after the Whitsuntide play, where Stephen hopes to encounter E— C— on the steps.

> He left the stage quickly and rid himself of his mummery and passed out through the chapel into the college garden. Now that the play was over his nerves cried for some further adventure. He hurried onwards as if to overtake it. The doors of the theatre were all open and the audience had emptied out. On the lines which he had fancied the moorings of an ark a few lanterns swung in the night breeze, flickering cheerlessly. He mounted the steps from the garden in haste, eager that some prey should not elude him, and forced his way through the crowd in the hall and past the two jesuits who stood watching the exodus and bowing and shaking hands with the visitors. He pushed onward nervously, feigning a still greater haste and faintly conscious of the smiles and stares and nudges which his powdered head left in its wake.
>
> When he came out on the steps he saw his family waiting for him at the first lamp. In a glance he noted that every figure of the group was familiar and ran down the steps angrily.
>
> —I have to leave a message down in George's Street, he said to his father quickly. I'll be home after you.
>
> Without waiting for his father's questions he ran across the road and began to walk at breakneck speed down the hill. (85–86)

There is much potential for color, movement, and drama in the

Whitsuntide play and the scenes surrounding it, from Heron's whipping of Stephen's legs to Stephen's humiliating encounter with the "familiar" group on the steps. But the pictures, however skilfully drawn, are all subordinated to the story line, and the most dramatic scenes are hardly visualized. In the climactic scene right after the play, the only items actually pictured—and not pictured very sharply—are the "few lanterns" that "swung in the night breeze, flickering cheerlessly." There is an ulterior narrative reason for their presence: to undercut Stephen's enthusiasm and foreshadow the ordinary, cheerless reality he will soon encounter. But we do not see the stage, the mummery he takes off, the chapel, the garden, the doors of the theater, the empty hall, the two Jesuits (except for a generalized bowing and shaking of hands), the steps—or a single detail of the familiar group. To make the contrast between the two step scenes more graphic, define the visual elements that distinguish the later description, and focus the sharp movements of the narrative eye, let me present it shot by shot with some accompanying commentary:

1. The *quick light shower* had drawn off, tarrying in *clusters of diamonds* among the *shrubs of the quadrangle* where an exhalation was breathed forth by the *blackened earth*. (Sharp and concrete image of shower, which is *there* in the narrative even though not *there* in the scene, followed by literary metaphor and personification held in check by the shrubs of the quadrangle and the blackened earth.) *Cut to* close-up:

2. Their *trim boots prattled* as they stood on the *steps of the colonnade*. (The near idealization of the first shot is cut off sharply by a close-up of prattling trim boots on the colonnade steps; note that we are shown only a fragment of the figures and of the steps.) *Cut to*:

3. *talking quietly and gaily* (Another jump-cut, fragmenting the narrative picture, and another close-up fragment focusing on mouths.) *Cut to*:

4. *glancing at the clouds* (Camera tracks back slightly and follows the movement of their heads as they turn toward the sky.) *Cut to*:

5. *holding their umbrellas at cunning angles* against the *few last raindrops* (Close-up limited to the pattern of the umbrellas, against which a few raindrops fall.)

6. *closing them* again (Same as 5, the pattern developing into a new stage.)

7. *holding their skirts demurely* (Same as 5, the narrative eye tilting slightly to focus on the skirts.)

The narrative eye captures a great amount of detail; note the proportion of italicized words. It moves swiftly from point to point, fragmenting the scene as a whole. It is aroused by details for their own intrinsic value rather than for the sake of the story. And it seizes not only on details but on formal patterns, which become as important as the details that compose them. This singular narrative picture reflects the development of Stephen's mind on a level different from—or in contrast to—the levels upon which he theorizes or self-consciously imagines.

Margaret Church establishes this development as she compares Joyce's concepts of the epiphany to the Viconian *ricorso*: "a moment—a period—when old things fall apart, disintegrate, and when with eyes burning 'with anguish and anger' one sees the vain illusions of one's life laid bare and there is no where to go, except, phoenix-like to be reborn . . . the flash of lightning . . . a kind of electrical shock to process, shattering it and provoking at the same time new process."[10] In the last chapter of *Portrait*, Stephen is still the self-conscious artist *manqué*, inhibited by the mask of his wit and the molds of literary fashion, and invoking new illusions as fast as he casts off the old ones. But he does begin to see as the artist should. The "flash of lightning," the "electric shock to process," the "shattering" constitute the dynamics of his epiphany.

In both the early novel, where picturing is subordinate to telling, and the novel where reality is a measure of objective perception, the narrative eye moves with regularity. It either selects details to advance the plot, establish a mood, focus the symbolism; or it turns mechanically from right to left, top to bottom, front to rear. The narrative pictures in the first four chapters of *Portrait* are in this sense traditional. In the last chapter Stephen begins to see. And the narrator, reflecting the development of his consciousness (although at times ironically), engages us in the act of seeing. The narrative eye does not compose what it has seen before: it is aroused by what it is seeing for the first time. It scans the field, flashing from point to point to discover individuating and meaningful patterns. And the movement of the searching eye begins to compete with the movement of the story—that is, the movement of the protagonist as he goes from one place and one stage of life to another. But unlike the movement of realist panning, it does not level what is seen. Quite the contrary, it discovers details that are unique—that are intrinsically interesting or subjectively attractive. It brings thought, images of the past, into the present. It fragments wholes to realize the value of parts and forms singular patterns.

The picture of the girls on the library steps is more radical than any other picture in *Portrait*. The narrative eye moves faster, shifts its position from far to near, changes its angle from wide to narrow, fragments so sharply that details like the trim boots are completely cut off from the girls to whom they belong and become an independent source of interest, and brings into focus kinetic patterns that are purely pictorial. As a result we are engaged in the dynamics of seeing, and also in the dynamics of composition. So in his first novel, Joyce develops from traditional to phenomenal to what we might call modernist picturing—where the medium, our most immediate point of contact, directly stimulates the sensation of movement and calls attention to itself in the process. In *Ulysses* the movement of the narrative eye and many other elements of the novel's medium will not only engage us directly but take on a dramatic life of their own and become a gratuitous force. But before we turn to the first novel in motion, let us take a chronological leap to a writer whom Joyce influenced. William Faulkner did not go as far as Joyce in imparting motion to all the elements of the medium. But he did develop the movement of the narrative eye with singular range and power as it tries to grasp the senselessness of his world.

CHAPTER THREE

Reeling through Faulkner

The narrator of Joyce's *Portrait* looks with sympathy and irony through the eyes of Stephen Dedalus, sometimes pulling back to undermine what Stephen says or feels, but never becoming involved. Faulkner's narrator, on the contrary, is always involved. Amazed and outraged at the energy that drives his characters to creative and destructive ends, his narrative eye is in continual motion, and this motion becomes central to his most powerful novels. Of course, Faulkner was affected by a sense of movement that Joyce had only begun to experience—the development of the automobile and the airplane, the increased restlessness and social as well as physical mobility (especially in America), cubism, futurism, jazz—and, of course, the movies. Indeed, Faulkner worked in the movies, although his film scripts were far less cinematic than his novels.[1] And moving pictures will provide a key to his kinetic power.

When Faulkner arrived in Hollywood in May of 1932, he was all ready to start writing. "I've got an idea for Mickey Mouse," he told Sam Marx of Metro-Goldwyn-Mayer. Faulkner would never write the Mickey Mouse script, which "Marx gently informed him . . . were written at the Walt Disney Studios";[2] but he had already indulged his impulse by cartooning the likes of Byron Snopes, Jason Compson, Anse Bundren, Eupheus Hines, and Popeye. He would continue to realize it in the variety of characters who run, hunt, gallop, fly, raid, chase, and escape throughout his novels.

Mickey Mouse, in the late twenties and thirties, was not the cute figure he would become, nor had his creator's imagination yet sighted on Disneyland. Movement, as Erwin Panofsky points out, is what generated the universal interest in film—"the sheer delight in the fact that things seem to move, no matter what they were."[3] Disney realized the comic and fantastic possibilities of movement in the speed of his chases, the speed of Mickey's wit, and the speed of his film's imaginative and surreal transformations.

Disney, of course, was not the first or most important artist to exploit the possibilities of movement. Cubism with its shifting perspectives, jazz with its syncopation, silent film with Griffith's last-minute rescue and Eisenstein's montage—all thrived on motion and seeded new possibilities.[4] Faulkner was attracted to the *pictures of motion* in Disney's cartoons—the stylized running, driving, flying, chasing, and escaping. His novels also reflect what we might call the *pictures in motion* that artists and filmmakers had developed to realize the possibilities of movement in their mediums. Both kinds of motion inform the dynamic and disturbing vision that Faulkner was evolving when he arrived in Hollywood in 1932.

PICTURES OF MOTION, PICTURES IN MOTION

Faulkner's first attempt at a Yoknapatawpha County novel begins with old man Falls recalling less a story than an ideal vision—of the original John Sartoris as he pretends to be a lame cracker and escapes from a Yankee search party:

> Cunnel says that was the hardest thing he ever done in his life, walkin' on thar acrost that lot with his back to'ads that Yankee without breakin' into a run. . . . Then the Yank hollered at him, but Cunnel kep right on, not lookin' back nor nothin'. Then the Yank hollered agin and Cunnel says he could hyear the hoss movin' and he decided hit was time to stir his shanks. He made the corner of the barn jest as the Yank shot the fust time, and by the time the Yank got to the corner, he was in the hawg-lot, a-tearin' through the jimson weeds to'ads the creek whar you was waitin' with the stallion hid in the willers. (4–5)[5]

A similar vision is recapitulated by Aunt Jenny of the original Bayard, after a successful attack on a Yankee stronghold—as he galloped back for a can of anchovies: "He rode yelling 'Yaaaiiiih, Yaaaiiiih,' " with all the Yankees shooting at him, "right up the knoll and jumped his horse over the breakfast table and rode it into the wrecked commissary tent, and a cook who was hidden under the mess stuck his arm out and shot Bayard in the back with a derringer" (19).

Aunt Jenny's story is not just an expression of outrage at her brother's foolish and ignominious death. No more so than Gail Hightower's obsessive vision in *Light in August* of his grandfather galloping with a handful of men through a hundred miles of enemy territory, setting fire to a warehouse full of food, and then getting killed stealing a woman's chickens. For to Jenny, as she sits with John and the Scottish engineer before the sparking fire and thinks in images that would become more fully developed in the mind of Gail Hightower, "Bayard Sartoris' brief career swept like a shooting star across the dark plain of their mutual remembering and suffering, lighting it with a transient glare like a soundless thunder-clap, leaving a sort of radiance when it died"(19).

All three visions idealize bravado expressed in movement for its own sake—escaping, chasing, raiding—and Faulkner seizes on the form of cartoon characterization as well as on the cartoon chase to shape the ideal and embody its senseless energy. Movement for its own sake is expressed in its most fully cartoonlike form in *Pylon*, where a two-dimensional group of flyers attract large crowds with their mindless irresponsibility as well as their genuine and imaginative freedom, and where the entire novel is dominated by patterns of movement.[6] But the ideal of movement for its own sake is also expressed in visions most noted for their pastoral qualities. The deer in "The Old People" that Sam Fathers salutes as "Chief . . . Grandfather" stops only for an instant, "then its muscles suppled, gathered. It did not even alter its course, not fleeing, not even running, just moving with that winged and effortless ease . . . " (*Go Down, Moses,* 184). And if Old Ben appears to Ike "immobile, fixed in the green and windless noon's hot dappling" (209), what characterizes the bear in Ike's imagination and in reality is its power and speed. Old Ben "sped .. . with the ruthless and irresistible deliberation of a locomotive. . . . It ran in his knowledge before he ever saw it" (193). When he did see it, "it rushed through rather than across the tangle of trunks and branches as a locomotive would, faster than he had ever believed it could have moved" (211).

Very few of Faulkner's images are as immobile as the image Ike preserves of Old Ben in their ideal encounter. Although the concept of arrested motion, which Faulkner claims to have been his goal,[7] has been developed by so many sensitive critics to illuminate Faulkner's fiction, it has also effectively suppressed a palpable dimension of the experience. Take, for instance, the images of the abandoned sawmill in the pastoral opening of *Light in August* and of Rosa Coldfield, immobile in her straight-backed chair in the beginning of *Absalom, Absalom!*

Some of the machinery would be left, since new pieces could always be bought on the installment plan—gaunt, staring, motionless wheels rising from mounds of brick rubble and ragged weeds with a quality profoundly astonishing, and gutted boilers lifting their rusting and unsmoking stacks with an air stubborn, baffled and bemused upon a stump-pocked scene of profound and peaceful desolation, unplowed, untilled, gutting slowly into red and choked ravines beneath the long quiet rains of autumn and the galloping fury of vernal equinoxes. (2)

. . . and opposite Quentin, Miss Coldfield in the eternal black which she had worn for forty-three years now, whether for sister, father, or nothusband none knew, sitting so bolt upright in the straight hard chair that was so tall for her that her legs hung straight and rigid as if she had iron shinbones and ankles, clear of the floor with that air of impotent and static rage like children's feet. . . . (7)

These are images not of arrest but of resisting arrest. They are animated by the same kind of surprising energy that generates Disney's comic-surreal transformations. Machinery is gaunt, staring, astonished, stubborn, baffled, bemused. Motionless wheels rise from the rubble, gutted boilers lift their stacks, unplowed land guts into choked ravines. Energy is activated by the descriptive verbals: by the staring, rising, astonishing, lifting, rusting, unsmoking, gutting, baffled, bemused, unplowed, untilled. The many negatives, or words that attempt to deny motion, only serve to dramatize its potency: motionless wheels are wheels that could move, unsmoking stacks are stacks that should smoke, untilled and unplowed land is land that waits to be plowed and tilled. Rosa, holding herself in, is like a spring about to be released. Her picture too is animated by verbals and a significant negative—nothusband. In both descriptions (Rosa's is three times the length of my excerpt), sentences run on as if the objects resist being arrested by their syntax.

Faulkner's descriptions may be *of motion*—when they focus on races, raids, hunts, chases, and escapes and portray movement for its own sake. Or they may be *in motion*—when the subject is static and a sense of movement is imparted by the medium. The movement in his pictures of the static sawmill and immobile Rosa is evoked by the words that animate their referents and by the long sentences stretching to contain them.

Sometimes motion is imparted by a movement between sentences or parts of sentences—which become narrative-pictorial units—that is like the movement between shots of a film sequence. A film sequence is formed by a series of shots, or uninterrupted camera "takes." The film-maker not only captures his moving subject with the lens of his camera but moves the camera from shot to shot, sometimes closing in, sometimes pulling away, sometimes at a speed and angle quite different from those of the subject. A similar movement is effected through the transitions from shot to shot—the cuts, fades, and dissolves. Here is a moving picture of Dilsey, Faulkner's most composed character, from the most stable section of *The Sound and the Fury*. In order to focus its narrative-pictorial units, I will transcribe it into something like a shot-by-shot film scenario. To call attention to the movement within each unit, I will italicize the action verbs and verbals. To illuminate the movement between units, I will comment in the adjacent column.

1. The day *dawned* bleak and chill.

A *moving* wall of grey light out of the northeast	At the beginning of this long incomplete sentence, the dawn turns into a moving wall.
which, instead of *dissolving* into moisture, seemed to *disintegrate* into minute and venomous particles,	"Instead" is one of Faulkner's *negatives* that allows him to give us an image and take it away, but it nonetheless remains or fades as in a lap-dissolve. "Venom" adds a *new quality* or derives from a *new perspective*.
like dust	Another new quality and perspective is added through the simile.
that, when Dilsey *opened* the door of the cabin and *emerged, needled* laterally into her flesh,	Dust changes into particles that needle laterally; what might be called a *moving mixed metaphor* develops still another transformation or shift in perspective.
precipitating not so much a moisture as a substance partaking of the quality of thin, not quite congealed oil.	Now particles become a moisture again, negated and then transformed into not quite congealed oil.

2. The gown *fell* gauntly from her shoulders, across her fallen breasts, then *tightened* upon her paunch, and *fell* again, *ballooning* a little above the nether garments

   This sentence works like a series of shots moving down Dilsey's body. The movement is achieved within almost every shot by the verb, and between each shot by the connectives that reflect the *traveling eye of the narrator.*

3. which she *would remove* layer by layer as the spring *accomplished* and the warm days, in colour regal and moribund.

   Another kind of movement is effected through time and tense shift.

4. She had been a big woman once, but now her skeleton *rose, draped* loosely in unpadded skin that *tightened* again upon a paunch almost dropsical,

as though muscle and tissue had been courage or fortitude which the days or the years had consumed until only the indomitable skeleton was left *rising* | Muscle and tissue become personified, then unpersonified to be consumed.

The skeleton rises.

like a ruin | And becomes a ruin.

or a landmark | And then a landmark.

above the somnolent and impervious guts, | And finally the guts become impervious in this wildly moving mixture of metaphors, or shifting of perspectives.

and above that the collapsed face that gave the impression of the bones themselves being outside the flesh, *lifted* into the *driving* day with an expression at once fatalistic and of a child's astonished disappointment, | By now the shifts and transformations are coming so fast, no single picture of Dilsey holds together.

until she *turned* and *entered* the the house again. | Until she makes her second actual movement in this page-long moving picture. (281–82).

Besides Faulkner's stylized *pictures of motion*, then, are his *pictures in motion*. And his *pictures in motion* take two forms, which may be compared to the movement *within* and *between* film shots. Movement *within* the narrative-pictorial unit is evoked by Faulkner's long sentences that strive to contain their subjects, by the animation and personification of objects, by the verbals that convey motion as they define and describe, and by the negatives that imply potency. Movement *between* narrative-pictorial units is effected through the traveling narrative eye (Dilsey 2), moving mixed metaphors that transform the subject and shift perspectives (Dilsey 1 and 4), and the shifting of temporal perspectives (Dilsey 3).

THE HOVERING NARRATOR

This leads us to the role of the narrator who is looking at his subject and trying to grasp it. For although *pictures of motion* are what the narrator sees, *pictures in motion* are how the narrator sees; and, as I have tried to show, even when Faulkner is considered most objective—or detached—and omniscient, his narrator is engaged and limited. Limited in his capacity to grasp, hold, comprehend, accommodate the senselessness that drives his characters to destructive as well as heroic ends, his mind's eye is in constant motion. And the motion of the narrative eye becomes the subject of his most powerful novels.

The Sound and the Fury may have begun with a clear, coherent "mental picture . . . of the muddy seat of a little girl's drawers."[8] But though Caddy is central, she never appears in the narrative present. She affects the present: she is identified with every object in Benjy's world, she is responsible for every move on Quentin's last day, she causes all of Jason's frustrations. But her effects are the result of her absence, and her absence is the subject of each character's thoughts. The actual subject of the novel, however, is the approaches to Caddy and all the values identified with her. It is the four different approaches, or perspectives, and it is the movement from one perspective to another in a pattern that decomposes chronological, logical, and causal order. Indeed, this movement is accentuated in the section that has been considered the most stable—where the narrator is not detached and objective but hovering and engaged, first in the vicinity of Dilsey's consciousness as he tries to grasp it, then somewhere between Dilsey and Jason as he focuses on the climax of Jason's chase in a way that parallels Dilsey's stately walk to church, and finally where he draws the two disparate lines together in an enigmatic scene— as Jason leaps across the town square and brutally swings the carriage around to stop Benjy's screaming and restore an order that though stabilizing is nonetheless arbitrary. Still, the chronological, logical, and causal order that has been decomposed tends to reassert itself: the novel asks the reader to reconstruct a pattern that can be reconstructed.

In *As I Lay Dying*, with the exception of Addie's chapter, the temporal order is straightforward. But the perspective shifts so often and so fast—fifty-nine times among fifteen points of view— that the movement between narrative units continually upsets our equilibrium. Moreover, the movement is more complex, for each section is composed of a double perspective. It is not the narrow-minded, self-centered, and puritanic Cora who sees Addie's eyes "like two candles when you watch them gutter down into the sockets of iron candle-sticks" (8), especially as this image reappears in the Darl section just before Addie dies—"the two flames glare up for a steady instant"(47). It is not Vardaman who thinks about "the dark . . . resolving him out of his integrity, into an unrelated scattering of components"(55). Tull would hardly play with the pun on "bore," which relates the holes bored into Addie's face with the burdens borne by Anse and Cora (70). Nor would Darl—despite his natural sensitivity and lively imagination—be capable of the abstract and poetic thought and the feeling for language that pervade his sections; for there is nothing in the novel to suggest that he ever heard or read any more than what was available to his provincial family, and all he brought back from his service in France seems to have been a spyglass containing "a woman and a pig with two backs and no face"(244).

Added, then, to the view of the dominant character in each section is the view of the narrator who hovers nearby. Added to the kaleidoscopic intercutting from one perspective to another is the hovering of the narrator between his character's view and his own.[9] And added to the linear but ironic movement of the Bundrens—as they pass through fire and flood to destroy rather than integrate the family and replace Addie with a new Mrs. Bundren—is the gratuitous intercutting, or movement for its own sake, that continually fractures the story line.

PASSING THE STORY

Faulkner's impulse toward the hovering narrator may have been grounded in the southern tradition of storytelling and his own gift as a storyteller, as well as his compulsion to grasp the senseless pattern of history. His initial attempts to relate perspectives take the form of stories told by Falls, Simon, and Jenny in *Flags in the Dust* or *Sartoris*—which function as flashbacks and oscillate between the past and present. The flashback, or intercutting from story to story, adds the movement of the cutting to the movement of the story. This movement is most suited to the chase, which in one form or another dominates Faulkner's novels as well as the silent film and the cartoons that so delighted him.

In *Light in August* Faulkner develops a story of multiple chases—a hectic picture of motion—as well as a disturbing experience of unpredictable movement—or picture in motion— through an intercutting of stories, the gratuitous passing of the story from one storyteller to another throughout all but that section of the novel recounting what no one in Jefferson could know about Christmas. Although the cutting is not so fast as that in *As I Lay Dying,* the range of perspectives and storytellers is far wider and the total experience is far more unsettling.

It is more unsettling, first, because the picture of motion is far less clear. Rather than the simple movement from home to city, *Light in August* is composed of varying kinds of chases and escapes. Lena chases Brown with tranquil confidence. Byron chases Lena with stumbling awkwardness. Christmas escapes from the posse with the comic ingenuity of the early Mickey Mouse. McEachern galloping straight to the dance hall he had never heard of, Hines riding straight out to find Milly and the circus man, and Percy Grimm cooly pursuing Christmas through the chessboard of Jefferson's alleys and streets—all chase their quarries with uncanny certainty. Brown is continually on the run to escape identity. And Christmas continually escapes to discover one.[10]

Added to the multiplicity of pace and direction—to the picture of motion—is the oscillation of the hovering narrator and the passing of the story from one storyteller to another. Indeed, these two kinds of movement become related, for, as I will try to show, the experience of the novel is dominated by both the oscillation and the succession of perspectives.

Part of the story is told by a narrator who focuses on the consciousness of Lena, Byron, Hightower, and principally Joe Christmas. Indeed, he tells Christmas's story from the ritualistic preparation for Joanna's murder, or the act that was to give Christmas an identity as the "nigger murderer," back to his first consciousness of identity in the orphanage, and then straight along those "savage and lonely streets"(207) that led to Joanna's and the murder. Other parts of the story are told by various storytelling characters. Byron, the principal storyteller, tells parts of the Lena and Christmas stories to Hightower. Joanna's story about Calvin and Nathaniel Burdens interrupts the narrator's story about Christmas. Mrs. and Mr. Hines pass along the story of Milly and Christmas's birth. Various townspeople describe the chase, and a collective, choric persona—"the clerks, the idle, the countrymen in overalls; the talk"—tells the story of Christmas's capture (330 ff.). Gavin Stevens is brought into the novel only for his interpretive narration of the climax, which he has not even witnessed, and the furniture dealer tells his wife a funny story about Byron and Lena as they leave Jefferson.

Although the voices of the storytelling characters are often more clearly defined than those in *As I Lay Dying*, intercut into them nonetheless is the awe, amazement, disbelief, rage, irony, and sympathetic humor of the hovering narrator. Further, some stories—like that of the posse chasing Christmas—are passed along and developed by one storyteller after another; and some stories are passed along and retold by different storytellers: we hear about the fire and the murder three times each, and the story of Christmas's death is retold after Gavin Stevens tells it by the narrator, who draws back to see it from the viewpoints of Christmas and Grimm and finally the townspeople. To suggest the kind of picture in motion generated by *Light in August,* let me trace the passing of the story in its exposition.

The novel begins with the story of Lena Grove, told from her viewpoint; but the narrative oscillates between her innocent musings, as she passes through the tranquil countryside, and the perceptions of the narrator—who knows how she fits, or does not fit, into the violent story that follows, and who projects his violent ambiguity into the descriptions of the sawmill, the train, and the wagon. Soon there is a shift to the perspective of Armstid and the countrymen, which, remaining within the pastoral setting, gives us an outsider's and a man's view of Lena. Here the narrator intrudes only to provide an ironic focus on the countrymen's folk wisdom.[11] But as Lena comes within sight of Jefferson, sees the smoke from Joanna's burning house but thinks only of how long she has been on the road, there is a radical break in the story line, an unanticipated intercutting from one subject to another—a sudden leap from country to city and into the consciousness of a new character focusing on another new character, and a sudden shift in pace, mood, and import.

"Byron Bunch knows this" (27), we are told with categorical finality. What he knows—but what the hovering narrator knows better as he adds his perceptions and wit to Byron's naïve and plodding mentality—is how two strangers came to the mill several years before: Joe Christmas, with his "stiffbrim straw hat . . . cocked at an angle arrogant and baleful above his still face" (27), and Joe Brown, who is supposed to have put Byron "in mind of one of these cars running along the street with a radio in it. You can't make out what it is saying and the car ain't going anywhere in particular and when you look at it close you see that there ain't even anybody in it"(32-33).

Soon the story passes on to a new consciousness, and we discover what the Reverend Gail Hightower knows about Byron; that is, we are told what Byron has told Hightower, which Hightower but not Byron knows is about Byron falling in love. Then, as we watch Hightower sitting at his window, "waiting for that instant when all light has failed out of the sky" (55), we hear what

Byron heard when he first came to town—or the story the towns-people told Byron about Hightower. Finally we are presented with a dramatic scene of Byron and Hightower facing each other, but the scene is set for still another story, or another telling of the same story—of Lena's arrival in Jefferson, the discovery of Joanna's body, and the posse starting after Christmas.

In the first seventy pages of the novel, the story has been passed along six times. Twice it is a part of the story that has been told to the storyteller before. Twice we hear of Lena's arrival at the saw-mill. Three times we see the fire of Joanna's burning house. It is only on the seventy-first page that we begin to feel that the various parts of the story, which have been told out of sequence as well as repeatedly, begin to shape themselves into a coherent pattern. But there is no connection between the two parts of the story Byron tells Hightower as they face each other in the lamplight. His tale of Lena leads up to her asking, "Is he still enough of a preacher to marry folks?"—that is, to marry Lena and Brown. Hightower then asks, "What is this you are telling me?" What Byron answers is that "Christmas is part nigger." And this leads to the story of finding Joanna's body and the beginning of the chase (82–83).

We may be able to reason a connection between the two parts of Byron's story, since Lena arrived in Jefferson as Joanna's house was burning and her lover had been living in Joanna's cabin with Christmas. But the connection we are made to feel derives from the breathless pace of the narrative as it leaps from one consciousness to another back and forth in time. Or it derives from the desperate motion of the narrator's consciousness as he shifts perspectives—now hovering near the mind of one character, now cutting from one storyteller to another—trying to grasp the connections and contain the senseless motion of his world. That he can never grasp the connections or contain the motion is expressed in the pace of his narrative, in the level of intensity to which he raises all the narrative voices, and in the discontinuous shifts in perspective. It is ultimately expressed in the Hightower chapter, which succeeds the climax of Christmas's death contrary to our expectations, and in the gap between the central story and the pastoral frame.

The dominant image in the Hightower chapter is of the wheel, but the wheel is not introduced as an object of Hightower's thoughts. Rather, it is a simile, an object of the narrator's own imagination that serves to describe what he sees in Hightower's evolving consciousness: "Thinking begins to slow now. It slows like a wheel beginning to run in the sand" (462). The wheel continues as the narrator's simile and metaphor, becoming an instrument of torture, as Hightower feels the pain of his growing awareness. Even when the wheel is released—"going fast and smooth now, because it is freed now of burden, of vehicle, axle, all"—and gives way to the halo, it is still a simile: "In the lambent suspension of August . . . it seems to engender and surround itself with a faint glow like a halo"(465). This simile, though, serves as a bridge from the narrator's to Hightower's direct consciousness, for in the next sentence the halo does not *seem like* but *is* "full of faces . . . peaceful, as though they have escaped into an apotheosis." Hightower's vision of ultimate unity is seen by the reader firsthand; indeed, it is shared by Hightower, the narrator, and the reader, thereby extending the experience of unity to the limits of the novel. But this unity is immediately destroyed—as one face dissolves into two, and the faces of Joe Christmas and Percy Grimm "seem to strive," not because they themselves are striving or desiring it, "but because of the motion and desire of the wheel itself"(465-66).

It is just this motion that the hovering narrator seeks to contain—a motion that seems to have no cause beyond itself and no purpose other than to keep on going. A motion that is idealized in the daring of the original John Sartoris and the original Gail Hightower, and that drove Christmas to reject the misfitting identities offered to him by a rigid society. But a motion too that led to the death of Sartoris and Hightower, to the senseless violence of the Civil War and World War I, and to the acts of negation—rejection and murder—that were the only means for Joe Christmas to say "I am."

Finally, the motion of Hightower's spinning wheel is succeeded by the motion of horsemen, sweeping past Hightower "with tumult and soundless yelling . . . like a tide whose crest is jagged with the wild heads of horses and the brandished arms of men like the crater of the world in explosion"(466-67). This is the motion of Hightower's consciousness, which continues beyond the moment of self-understanding and experience of unity, and even beyond his disturbing apprehension of what happened in Jefferson that day. It is also the motion of the narrative mind, which, unable to grasp the senseless and autonomous energy, again tries one simile after another and transforms the horsemen into a tide and then a crater.

If the novel's ending is pastoral, and if Lena is the epitome of composure, the jump-cut between the last two chapters accentuates and extends the senseless *picture in motion*. And if the narrator finally adds his gentle irony to the voice of the furniture dealer and extends a note of sympathy to Byron, he leaves us with a picture of Byron still in pursuit of Lena, even as they sit together in a truck carrying them to no particular destination—"watching the telephone poles and fences passing like it was a circus parade" (480). The ending of the novel might complete the pastoral frame that surrounds the central violence, and it might offer an alternative to that violence—although not one available to modern man and woman. But, as I have tried to show, the principle governing *Light in August* is one of continual movement and senseless succession. Although the story passes from storyteller to storyteller, shifts perspectives, violates chronology, and repeats itself in different ways, it is continually driven forward. Indeed, the dislocations and discontinuities are felt only because of the novel's forward motion. Here too the model of a film sequence will help us understand the essentially narrative element that Faulkner develops. One shot of a moving picture may succeed another in a way that violates continuities of space or time, but it nonetheless succeeds it. Movement is the basis of narrative in film and fiction, and succession is the basis of narrative movement. What is so disturbing about Faulkner's view of the world is that the succession seems ungoverned and ungovernable—that the motion, which inspires heroism, avarice, and violence, derives only from itself and leads to apocalypse. This is the picture of motion in Faulkner's most powerful novels; the power derives from its full realization as a picture in motion.

Faulkner was satisfied with the galleys of *Light in August*, which he read shortly after he arrived in Hollywood. He told Sam Marx that Metro-Goldwyn-Mayer would not find *Sanctuary* suitable—though "it would make a good Mickey Mouse picture."[12] In his own way Faulkner was realizing in *Light in August* the possibilities of motion in pictures and pictures in motion that the silent film makers had developed and that was magnified in the Mickey Mouse cartoons. By extending the resources of the comic-surreal chase in the movement of his characters and of the cutting between perspectives in the movement of his narrative eye, he was able to engage us in a singular but multidimensional experience of what Henry Adams had symbolized in the American dynamo and what Thomas Pynchon would point to as entropy. In *Absalom,*

Absalom! he would develop the impulses that gave rise to *The Sound and the Fury* and *As I Lay Dying* through what I will compare to Eisenstein's montage, including within his compass the senseless movement of classical and biblical history. In *Go Down, Moses* he would seek out the earliest American source of his vision and introduce us into his most ambiguous picture of race relations with a racing and chasing in "Was" that could come right out of the early Disney. In the Snopes trilogy and *The Reivers*, as his rage would give way to tolerance and his ambiguity to humor, the vitality of his characters might have derived directly from the energetic, sharp-witted, imaginative, and winning Mickey Mouse.

CHAPTER FOUR

From Joyce to Beckett:
The Tale That Wags the Telling

ULYSSES

" 'Look!' " said James Joyce to Frank Budgen, as their conversation in a small Paris cafe was "interupted by the fierce pounding of an electric piano. . . . 'That's Bella Cohen's pianola. What a fantastic effect! All the keys moving and nobody playing.' "[1] Bella Cohen's pianola playing itself presents to our imagination two signal features. First, we become aware of the pianola as an active element in the musical experience rather than simply the instrument, or medium, that conveys it. Second, we become aware of the pianola, or medium, as what generates the musical experience—all the keys moving and nobody playing. In *Ulysses* Joyce causes us to see not only what happens to Stephen and Bloom and what their world looks like but what the material that composes their world looks like as well. He brings the medium of the novel into its dramatic compass, gives his medium the same kind of dramatic life he gives his characters. He also makes it into a dynamic force that threatens his characters and continually upsets the equilibrium of his readers. Like Bella Cohen's pianola, the medium of *Ulysses* is an active element in the experience we encounter; indeed, it is a formidable antagonist. It is also an autonomous, self-generating cause of what we encounter. What a fantastic effect!

I have taken *Ulysses* out of its chronological position in order to follow one course of the novel in motion that Joyce helped initiate—as the narrative eye becomes a dominant dramatic force. Joyce's picture of the girls on the library steps in *Portrait*—with its swift shifts in perspective, sharp fragmentation, and attention to gratuitous detail—foreshadows much in *Ulysses*, but even more in the novels of William Faulkner. In *Portrait* Joyce's narrator, identifying with Stephen Dedalus even when he views him ironically, engages us in the act of excited perception as Stephen learns to see. Faulkner goes a step further, for his pictures in motion are generated not by any character in the world of his novels but by the narrator, trying to apprehend the senseless energy that drives his characters to creative and destructive ends, and generating another level of senseless energy as he mediates between us and their stories. It is his mediation, then, that continually upsets our equilibrium and stimulates the sensation of motion. Or, to put it in another way, our sensation of motion derives from a major component of the narrative medium. In Joyce's *Ulysses* the narrator often identifies with a character and engages us in the act of excited perception, whether what we see is present in the character's world or in his mind. Sometimes he engages us in the act of seeing what his characters could not see. But he also engages us in the activity of his medium's other components: the shifting styles, the sounds of words, the look of words on the printed page, an arbitrary point of view, language issuing from no source in the narrative world and gathering its own momentum, stage directions and dialogue attributions. Every component of the novel's medium is brought into its dramatic compass. But they also intrude into the narrative, compete with what is happening, interfere with what we are trying to see and understand, and become the source of a new kind of movement that threatens and enlivens us.

We have looked with Stephen Dedalus across his "threadbare cuffedge" to see a "ring of bay and skyline" that "held a dull green mass of liquid," and within his mind to see the "bowl of white china . . . holding the green sluggish bile" torn up by his dying mother.[2] We have seen something, though not much, of Mr. Deasy's school and Sandymount strand. We have seen a great deal of Dublin through the eyes of Leopold Bloom, in scenes continually fragmented by his recollections and associations. Suddenly we encounter not a scene but a *page*—where what Bloom sees is fragmented by boldface headings. Indeed, what Bloom sees is only part of a pattern that includes—is in fact dominated by— the typography.

IN THE HEART OF THE HIBERNIAN METROPOLIS

BEFORE NELSON'S PILLAR, TRAMS SLOWED, SHUNTED, CHANGED TROLLEY started for Blackrock, Kingstown and Dalkey, Clonskea, Rathgar and Terenure, Palmerston park and upper Rathmines, Sandymount Green,

Rathmines, Ringsend and Sandymount Tower, Harold's Cross. The hoarse Dublin United Tramway Company's timekeeper bawled them off:

—Rathgar and Terenure!

—Come on, Sandymount Green!

Right and left parallel clanging ringing a doubledecker and a single-deck moved from their railheads, swerved to the down line, glided parallel.

—Start, Palmerston park!

THE WEARER OF THE CROWN

Under the porch of the general post office shoeblacks called and polished. Parked in North Prince's street His Majesty's vermilion mailcars, bearing on their sides the royal initials, E. R., received loudly flung sacks of letters, postcards, lettercards, parcels, insured and paid, for local, provincial, British and overseas delivery.

GENTLEMEN OF THE PRESS

Grossbooted draymen rolled barrels dullthudding out of Prince's stores and bumped them up on the brewery float. On the brewery float bumped dullthudding barrels rolled by grossbooted draymen out of Prince's stores.

—There it is, Red Murray said. Alexander Keyes.

—Just cut it out, will you? Mr. Bloom said, and I'll take it round to the *Telegraph* office.

The door of Ruttledge's office creaked again. Davy Stephens, minute in a large capecoat, a small felt hat crowning his ringlets, passed out with a roll of papers under his cape, a king's courier. (115)

It is only at the bottom of the page that we discover we are in a newspaper world, and that the boldface headings are like news-paper headlines. Still, we cannot locate their source. They are not part of what any character sees or thinks. Nor are they part of what the narrator sees or says. They are certainly not taken from any newspaper. The headlines are just *there*—gratuitous, ob-durate lines of boldface print that intrude into the narrative, in-terrupt, fragment, and sometimes focus or comment upon the scene. What we encounter in "Aeolus," besides what Bloom and Stephen see of the newspaper offices, is the medium, the very ma-terial that forms the novel. What we see on the screen of our visual imagination includes both the imaginary world of the newspaper offices and the tangible page of print. In "Aeolus" the medium has become a dramatic element, which David Hayman describes as a counterforce.[3] It has become a tangible antagonist against which the narrator, the characters, and the reader will have to contend. And it will become a driving force of the novel.

We continue to follow Stephen and Bloom in their aimless wanderings through the streets of Dublin, evolving a sense of their habits and needs. That is, we form a relatively coherent though complex picture of the novel's main characters. But we form this picture against the force of a narrative medium that grows increasingly arbitrary and at times almost opaque. For the narrative voice, having been playfully undermined in "Aeolus," is nearly overcome by the arbitrary musical sounds in "Sirens," blown all out of proportion by the "giganticism" of "Cyclops," nearly obscured by the stylistic parodies in "Oxen of the Sun." In "Circe" there is no conflict between the narrative voice and the counterforce of the medium: the narrative voice is completely usurped by a set of stage directions. Denied our narrative guide, we encounter the nighttown experience completely on our own: we have almost no way of telling the level of actual action and speech from the levels of recollection, daydreaming, fantasy, or deep unconscious projection. And here, where Bella Cohen's pianola appears as part of the nightmare, we can discern most clealy the medium's twofold role as tangible dramatic element and self-generating dramatic force.

> *The Mabbot street entrance of nighttown, before which stretches an uncobbled tram siding set with skeleton tracks, red and green will-o'-the-wisps and danger signals. Rows of flimsy houses with gaping doors. Rare lamps with faint rainbow fans. Round Rabaiotti's halted ice gondola stunted men and women squabble. They grab wafers between which are wedged lumps of coal and copper snow. Sucking, they scatter slowly. Children. The swancomb of the gondola, highreared, forges on through the murk, white and blue under a lighthouse. Whistles call and answer.*
>
> THE CALLS
>
> Wait, my love, and I'll be with you.
>
> THE ANSWERS
>
> Round behind the stable. (429)

What we first encounter in "Circe" is a set of stage directions. The nightmare is initiated by their coming to life. Flimsy houses gape at us. The swanscomb of Rabaiotti's ice gondola rears itself on high and forges through the murk. Whistles call and answer. But more: words are transformed into objects or stage props, and sound effects come to life. A will-o'-the-wisp, the name for an elusive and unseen creature, is a metaphor; but we are asked to see will-o'-the-wisps casually alternating with the danger signals that line the railroad tracks. The whistles' calls and answers are sound effects, but they are given lines of dialogue—"Wait, my love, and I'll be with you," call the whistles' calls. "Round behind the stable," answer the whistles' answers.

The stage directions and dialogue attributions not only come to life in the experience of nighttown, they are a dramatic force. It is the stage directions that cause Bloom to give birth to eight male yellow and white children, cover his left eye with his left ear, pass through several walls, hang on Nelson's pillar by his eyelids, eat twelve dozen oysters (shells included), eclipse the sun by extending his little finger. And while Bella Cohen might act the role of Circe, it is the costume changes that evoke the multiple transformations of character, or awaken sleeping personae. What I am trying to point out is that the dramatic script that intrudes itself into the narrative of *Ulysses* is not, like the conventional script, a set of directions for a theatrical performance (even though the nighttown scene has been staged and filmed). The effect of the episode would be lost if a director were to create something like a will-o'-the-wisp and have it stand or move among the danger signals, if we were to hear a whistle call, "Wait, my love," if we were to see Bloom give birth to eight male yellow and white children or hang from Nelson's pillar by his eyelids. The stage directions and dialogue attributions—the particular manifestations of the novel's medium in "Circe"—are not signals for action. They are elements of the drama. They are as much a part of the fully imagined experience as the characters, the background, the movement, the dialogue, the streams of consciousness. Moreover, they are major forces in the drama and generate its erratic movement; they directly affect the characters, create discontinuities, and cause a series of comic but disturbing conjunctions and collisions.

In the "Circe" episode the medium usurps the narrator. What the reader sees on the screen of his visual imagination is not a picture of characters talking, thinking, and acting against a surrealistic background—a picture, that is, contained within the narrator's consciousness and transmitted through his voice. Rather, the reader sees an erratic montage composed of subject matter and the materials of the printed language—characters, memories, fantasies, pieces of stage sets, words, and empty spaces—kept in continual motion, arbitrarily fragmented, senselessly joined, comically animated and impelled, like Bella Cohen's pianola, by the medium itself. What a fantastic effect: all the keys are moving and nobody is playing.

Let me try to elaborate on the dynamics of montage by employing another model, this time from Sergei Eisenstein's first film. In the year after Joyce published *Ulysses,* Eisenstein was producing Ostrovsky's play, aptly titled *Enough Simplicity in Every Sage.* He was inspired to fit into his dramatic production a short film, which, like Joyce's intrusion of the play script into his novel, had the alienating effect of mirroring characters, set, and action in another medium. Indeed, by speeding up the film, he could convey what Joyce conveyed less directly: characters impelled by the movement of the medium itself.

The play, as Eisenstein describes it in *Film Form,* is an elaborate intrigue in which Glumov deceives his uncle by courting his aunt, while at the same time deceiving the aunt by courting the niece. For the film insert Eisenstein made imaginative use of the stage set, which was shaped like a circus arena with a small raised platform at one end. He arranged for the scene with the uncle to take place downstage in the arena, and for the fragments with the aunt to take place on the platform. "Instead of changing scenes, Glumov . . . ran from one scene to the other and back—taking a fragment of dialogue from one scene, interrupting it with a fragment from the other scene—the dialogue thus colliding, creating new meanings and sometimes wordplays. Glumov's leaps acted as *caesurae* between the dialogue fragments."[4]

The key elements of Eisenstein's montage are caesura, leaping, fragment, and collision. Now let us see what we would imagine if Eisenstein's model were applied to "Circe." Joyce's stage set, like Eisenstein's, might be shaped like a circus arena, with a series of overlapping platforms at one end. The action that takes place between 12 and 1 A.M., in the grotesque present of Mabbot Street and Bella Cohen's whorehouse, would be played on the ground level of surreality. Fragments from the hallucinated past and future of Bloom and Stephen and of their literary analogues would be played on one or another of the raised platforms. Instead of changing scenes, Bloom, and to a lesser extent Stephen, would run from one scene to another—taking a fragment of dialogue from one scene, interrupting it with a fragment from another scene—the dialogue thus colliding, creating new meanings and sometimes wordplays. The leaps of Bloom and Stephen would act as caesurae between the dialogue fragments.

Frank Budgen has pointed out that Joyce composed *Ulysses* as a mosaic, and A. Walton Litz has described this process in detail.[5] But though both Budgen and Litz have contributed immeasurably to our understanding of Joyce's mode of composition, and their image of the mosaic accounts for the fragmentation as well as our awareness of the medium, it does not account for the two-fold role of the medium in *Ulysses* or the disorienting motion that engages us. For a mosaic, though composed of many fragments, is perceived as fragments situated next to one another in space and not following one another in time. Moreover, it is seen as a composition of static fragments cemented together. The medium, then, though part of what we encounter, does not generate the movement from one fragment to another which Eisenstein describes in terms of leaping and, especially, collision. Although film makers and critics have often discussed montage as the cementing together of film fragments, or shots, from the early days of cinematic art Eisenstein argued to the contrary. The key to montage, he insisted, is conflict; the relationship between film fragments is not the cemented joint but collision. Indeed, joining, he tells us, is only a special case of collision; for when two spheres collide, an infinite number of combinations may result. One of these combinations "is so weak that collison is degraded to an even movement of both spheres in the same direction."[6]

Joyce and Eisenstein recognized that they were "moving along kindred lines."[7] Although Joyce did not formulate his aesthetic principles in terms of montage or catalog them as systematically as Eisenstein did, the effects of *Ulysses* can be usefully described in Eisenstein's language, especially in terms of collision, which is the essence of Eisenstein's theory. I have tried to show how Joyce brought all the components of his medium into the dramatic compass of *Ulysses*, and how the self-generating dynamic of his medium becomes a driving force. Let me now try to show how the movement we encounter in *Ulysses* can be described as a series of collisions that both include the medium and are generated by it.

Collision of characters is the most obvious because it results in the special case of joining. We will immediately think of the joining of manifest characters: Stephen and Bloom, Molly and Martha, Gerty and Mrs. Purefoy. Or we will think of joining a character and his mythic counterpart: Bloom and Ulysses or Christ, Stephen and Telemachus or Hamlet. What is often lost in the intellectual exercise of discovering these kinds of links in *Ulysses* are the radical differences—the caesurae—that make themselves felt as one trait leads us to connect but others remain present to enforce the separation, the *leaps* our minds make and the feeling of continual oscillation that results from our not being able to land on one foot or the other, and the *collision* of associations we have with such different characters. To more fully represent the dynamics of this novel in motion would be to describe Stephen as leaping from the mundane world of twentieth-century Dublin to the world of Homer's *Odyssey* or Shakespeare's *Hamlet*, or of Bloom carrying fragments of his dialogue or interior monologue from 7 Eccles Street to Calypso's island or from Barney Kiernan's tavern to Cyclops's cave—and from the resulting collisions to describe the unsettling new meanings.

In one sense the collision of characters lies in the domain of the novel's subject matter: we are reading about Stephen, whose actions are parallel to Bloom's; we are reading about Bloom, whose journey is like Ulysses' and whose temperament is like Christ's. But we are made conscious of the connections by the reflexive form of the novel, by the medium, which forms connections that we know to be both meaningful and absurd. The second form of collision is more immediate and palpable. It comes when, straining to hear the narrator's voice or see his picture, we collide with an arbitrary style. We collide with the newspaper headlines in "Aeolus" as they undermine the narrator's voice and interrupt the action. We collide with the arbitrary pattern of sounds in "Sirens" as they distract us from following the complex choreography of characters in and out of Ormond's restaurant, and from following the multileveled stream of Bloom's consciousness just when he gives in irrevocably to becoming a cuckold. We collide with the literary parodies of "Oxen of the Sun" as they obfuscate the meeting of Stephen and Bloom that we have been anticipating for four hundred pages. Perhaps the most significant collision is between the reader and the catechistic style of "Ithaca," for here the style intrudes and transforms a quality of action—the long and important exchange between Stephen and Bloom—into a set of quantitative results. We can never see or hear what happens in the kitchen of 7 Eccles Street; we can only infer what happens through a process of addition. We cannot see a new relationship forming between Stephen and Bloom; we can only count up instances like Stephen's acceptance of Bloom's mustache cup. We cannot hear a conversation, which in contrast to that in "Eumaus" seems to have achieved a genuine dialogue; we can only infer how far Bloom and Stephen got with one another if they were led to discover such a "connecting link" as Mr. Riordan. We cannot directly feel the kind of male intimacy that developed between them; we can only deduce this from the fact that they playfully urinated together in the penumbra of Molly's lamp.

The capricious movement of the medium, as it collides with the reader, dislocates us from the scene of action. It is a force that keeps us from seeing, feeling, and knowing what happens during the most important moments in the story. And it is essentially comic in its surprise, incongruity, and power to create distance. When the medium gratuitously collides with the characters, it dislocates the reader and reveals its threatening potential. We first become aware of this collision in "Wandering Rocks," when we encounter an arbitrary shift in the point of view—and the dislocation is sensed before it is understood. Instead of focusing on the scene from the perspective of Stephen or Bloom, we are suddenly lifted, as it were, to a bird's-eye vantage; and we are engaged by a pattern of many characters moving through the streets of Dublin. More striking still, we see the major characters reduced to the same level of importance as a host of minor characters and, indeed, to a lower level of importance than some characters who are arbitrarily introduced for the first and last time. Moreover, the characters are fragmented; our dominant visual impression is of parts of people or their dress—Father Conmee's watch and silk hat, the sailor's single leg and crutch, Molly's arm, the carnation between Blazes Boylan's smiling teeth. What impels the movement in "Wandering Rocks" and reduces and fragments the characters is nothing more than the point of view. The counterforce as point of view collides with the characters, threatens them as free and integral human beings, and, continually dislocating the reader, keeps them beyond our grasp.

In "Cyclops" we are dislocated by two unrelated voices, the demotic voice that describes the naturalistic conflict between Bloom and the Dubliners, and the mock-heroic voice that transmogrifies this experience into gigantic proportions. But the mock-heroic voice, like the point of view in "Wandering Rocks," has no locus in the world of the novel. It is all style, language itself speaking and gathering momentum. When Bloom is threatened by the Dubliners on his return to the tavern and when he barely escapes the Citizen's biscuit tin, we feel an intensity of danger that emanates—not from the characters—but from the language that has gathered its momentun from a sheer accumulation of words. If the language, playing itself like the keys of Bella Cohen's pianola, creates one of the most comic effects in the novel, in its collision with Bloom it achieves its most menacing potential.

In the "Ithaca" episode the style is most threatening; and here we encounter the ultimate agon between Bloom and the medium. The language, now completely mechanical, not only transforms a quality of experience into a quantity of data: it threatens to reduce Bloom into one of the many countable items or objects. The threat is most potent right after Stephen leaves. Bloom, now completely alone for the first time during his long day, bumps his head on a walnut sideboard and is dramatically displaced by a long catalog of furniture in the front room.[8] Indeed, in the pages that follow, Bloom is reduced to one of the many objects. Throughout the day Bloom has been an alien object to the Dubliners in general and to Blazes in particular; he has been like the crumpled throwaway floating down the Liffey. If he seems to have survived the social and psychological threats, this is only because we have been allowed a sympathetic view into his consciousness. At the climax of his drama, the medium gratuitously imposes itself between us and Bloom, and we are left to focus on the agon between the novel's medium and the novel's main character. The achievement of *Ulysses* is that Bloom emerges as an individual who is uniquely humane and heroic. In his comic and realistic acceptance and affirmation of Molly's adultery and of his own situation, Bloom overcomes the threats not only of society, history, and his own psyche but of that ominous and anonymous force that Joyce locates in the very medium of his novel.

Still, the force is not brought under control, even though the "Ithaca" chapter is succeeded by Molly's soliloquy—where the medium no longer obtrudes, where there are no fragments, no leaps, no caesurae, and where the movement, though palpable, is continuous and cumulative. In the Molly chapter the printed page is almost transparent; the long sentences read easily and give rise to the sound of Molly's voice. In her unbroken monologue Molly draws together all her experience while centering on Bloom. The novel's conflicts are dispelled, and one source of conflict—the ungovernable medium—is subdued. But when we finish the chapter and put it into its total context, we do not feel a sense of equilibrium. There is a caesura between the last two chapters. Despite the superabundance of fact in the chapter that ends with Bloom going to sleep, we are not told of Bloom's asking for breakfast in bed: the signal request that impels Molly's monologue. There is a leap from the remote viewpoint in "Ithaca" to Molly's intimate and direct stream of consciousness. The Molly chapter then, though in itself harmonious and whole, is an element in the novel's dynamic montage; and if the medium is unobtrusive, it remains the driving force. Like Bella Cohen's pianola, all the keys are moving and nobody is playing.

SAMUEL BECKETT'S *WATT* AND HIS TRILOGY

Joyce's language in *Ulysses* has more than the power to call up Dublin on 16 June 1904 and embody the streams of its characters' consciousness. It becomes a fully autonomous element, issuing from no source within the narrative world and gathering its own momentum—a counterforce that is self-generating, arbitrary, intrusive, comic, and dramatically threatening. In Beckett it is not a counterforce but the only force. It does not intrude into the narrative world, it is all the world. It literally creates a world as one word after another fills in the empty space, and then it cancels what it has created. Or it creates a narrator who brings a world to life through his intercourse with the words he has written, who keeps from dying as long as he has lead in his pencil, and who is ultimately threatened by the very language he speaks. We know that Beckett was attracted by the fecundity of Joyce's language, especially in *Finnegans Wake*. If we turn to *Watt*, where he was beginning to find his own style, and the trilogy, where he fully realized it, we can see how he drew on the autonomous power of Joyce's language in *Ulysses*, how he endowed it with an even greater momentum, and how he realized its ultimately destructive potential.

On the opening page of *Watt*, Mr. Hackett turns a corner and sees, in the failing light, at some little distance, his seat. But what is the corner he turns? It is not like the stairhead from which Buck Mulligan emerges; we never see enough of the scene to place or define it. We do not even know—cannot even see—what it is the corner of. It has only a single dimension. It is no more than a point, an intersection, between what never was and what will become as one word succeeds another and fills up the page. It is the point from which Mr. Hackett emerges like a line drawing. First he is only a name, an abstraction, a virtual character. Then—as one verbal event follows another, and we follow the movement of the story line—the virtual becomes actual. Mr. Hackett stretches out his left hand and fastens it around a rail. Now that the rail is *there* to support his hand, he can strike his stick against the pavement and feel the thudding rubber in his palm. When he gets closer to the seat, the occupants appear part by part: "the lady held the gentleman by the ears, and the gentleman's hand was on the lady's thigh, and the lady's tongue was in the gentleman's mouth."[9] Even though the clauses of the sentence are joined by coordinating conjunctions, signifying the simultaneous presence of all the parts, we discover them one by one, incrementally. Each new element is a surprise. Mr. Hackett has called a policeman, although we do not discover this till he arrives, and he sees no indecency. After the lovers leave, Mr. Hackett can take his seat; and in his seat he emerges, part by part, until he is fully three-dimensional: "Mr. Hackett's nape rested against the solitary backboard, beneath it unimpeded his hunch protruded, his feet just touched the ground, the stick hooked around his neck hung between his knees" (9).

In *Watt* we are engaged in the extension of a story line—in its most concrete and elemental form. The opening section begins the process that extends through the whole length of the novel, for the story line—an autonomous, self-generating element—develops incrementally in two ways: first, as one word succeeds another; and, second, as one story succeeds another. A gentleman and a lady pass Mr. Hackett. They become husband and wife when the gentleman introduces Mr. Hackett. Then they become parents, Goff and Tetty Nixon, when they tell the story of Larry's birth. Larry is literally born and the husband and wife literally become parents in the telling of the story. Or, to put it another way, Larry exists as a character and they exist as his parents only in their story. This is just what happens in the body of the novel. Beckett's narrative strategy has been described in terms of combinations and permutations, but it is important to realize that each new combination and permutation is a new increment—a new movement, extending the story line as it extends the world of *Watt* into the empty space of the page. This movement is just what we experience when—to dispose of Mr. Knott's leftover food, on those occasions it is left over—the problem of a dog is considered. An average hungry or starving dog could hardly be expected to attend the house every evening between eight and ten for food that might not appear, so to solve the problem of a dog, the problem of its owner must be considered. The Lynch family appears—twenty-eight members afflicted by as many diseases and disabilities, each of which is accounted for in the twenty-six pages of extending story line.

So far as I know, every critic has accepted Sam as the ultimate storyteller, for Sam has taken careful notes from the time Watt began to "spin his yarn." Sam's mind is like Watt's and he is seeking to know Watt just as Watt was seeking to know Knott. He is obsessed by the same kinds of questions and generates the same incredible multiplicity of possibilities, and he brings into focus the nature of Watt's language—as well as the language Watt is constrained to compose in. "How hideous is the semi-colon" (158), he complains; and he is often forced to resort to question marks to make an ultimately enigmatic point. But what are we to make of those distinctly editorial interpolations: "Hiatus in MS" (238) and "MS illegible" (241)? Should they not lead us back to see the question marks and semicolon complaint as interpolations as well? If so, can the ultimate narrator really be Sam—at least the Sam who appears in the first person in the manuscript? If not, can we find any other voice in the novel to assure us of a narrative presence? No! What we have, from the first to the last page of *Watt*, is a story line extending itself, a yarn spinning itself out of empty space—bringing characters, objects, and events into existence through its own movement. The story line issues out of the empty space in the opening page, disappears in the empty space after tne Hackett section, turns Watt from a "roll of tarpaulin, wrapped up in dark paper and tied about the middle with a cord" (16) into a singular individual, burgeons out of the generative capacity of words as they succeed one another, comes nearly full circle—past where Sam sees Watt disappearing into the undergrowth for the last time—to where the train first took Watt to Mr. Knott's house. Watt is created out of the story line and is ultimately canceled by it, for we are finally left with the station attendants watching his train leave, looking from one to the other until Mr. Nolan looks "at nothing in particular, though the sky falling to the hills, and the hills falling to the plain, made as pretty a picture, in the early morning light, as a man could hope to meet with, in a day's march" (246). And then continuing through an appendix.

Watt is developed from a roll of tarpaulin into a singular individual by the movement of the story line, but Molloy is *there* from the very beginning—for Molloy tells his story in the first person. Molloy is in his mother's room. He is filling up empty pages with what he knows. Which is his story. What he knows, then—indeed, what he is—is what he writes. He knows nothing beyond his present situation. His present situation includes the words he has just written into the empty space. Whether they are in the past or present tense, they are presences. And it is through his engagement—through his toying, struggling, and intercourse —with these physical presences that his story comes to life.

He does not know how he got to his mother's room. He does not know whether his mother was dead when he arrived or only died later—that is, "enough to bury." He tells us, though, that he has taken her place. "I must resemble her more and more. All I need now is a son." And then Molloy gives birth to a son. Watch how: "Perhaps I have one somewhere. But I think not. He *would be* old now, nearly as old as myself. It *was* a little chambermaid. It *wasn't* true love" (my emphases).[10]

Molloy speculates upon the possibility, reflects upon the improbability—and then creates a son by shifting from the conditional present to the indicative (or actual) past: "He *would be* old now. . . . It *was* a little chambermaid." This grammaculate conception is also generated by a shift from "he" to "it." And though "it" has no antecedent in the text, we easily apprehend its referent, for such ellipses are common in everyday speech.[11] In this case "it" refers to the event of his son's conception—which is itself conceived by Molloy's pencil dallying with the grammar and filling in the empty space after a sentence defining his son as no more than what Stephen Dedalus called a "Godpossibled soul" (389).

Watt is the process of words, as autonomous physical presences, extending themselves into a story line, creating and finally canceling a world by the addition of new increments. *Molloy* is also the product of an autonomous, procreative language, but not of a burgeoning story line. Rather, it is a process we can understand more graphically by comparing it to Beckett's plays. Krapp listens to what he recorded in the past, but the words exist only in the present; their autonomous presence is made dramatically evident by their issuing from a tape recorder. And Krapp creates himself from moment to moment by reacting to the sounds he hears. In *Act without Words I*, Beckett's mime creates himself silently through his intercourse not with words but with objects: a carafe, a tree, a rope, and a pair of scissors. And Winnie creates perhaps the most memorable character on the modern stage through her verbal intercourse with the objects in her purse. So Molloy is challenged by, challenges, teases, laments over, and engenders new life out of the words he has just written—that are *there* on the page just as Krapp's sounds, the mime's objects, and Winnie's purse are *there* on the stage. He questions them, is disturbed by them, undermines or contradicts them, shifts their tense or mood, creates ellipses. He also engenders alternative characters by mitosis (Was it A or C? Lousse or Mrs. Loy? Edith or Ruth?), evinces surprise at what he creates ("Well, well, I didn't know I knew this story so well"[58]), and completely abandons many of his offspring.

Molloy creates his own elusive self by filling up the empty pages with words and interacting with them, continuously creating new presences and a new present. But he is also aware that the language he toys with has its own autonomous power and generates its own movement. "Saying is inventing. Wrong, very rightly wrong. You invent nothing, you think you are inventing, you think you are escaping, and all you do is stammer out your lesson" (32). We will not realize the full import of Molloy's intuition until we come to *The Unnamable*, where we will discover that the language of the trilogy, though seeming to be the product of one narrator after another, is not under their control—and that it excludes the possibility of their not only inventing but saying anything for themseves.

As we read through the trilogy, one storyteller yields to another. The second part of the first novel is narrated by Moran, who goes out in search of Molloy. Moran starts off as a conventional character speaking in a conventional voice, but he ends up looking and speaking like Molloy. He hears a voice telling him things. "It did not use the words that Moran had been taught. . . . It told me to write the report." The report—the novel—ends: "Then I went back into the house and wrote, It is midnight. The rain is beating on the windows. It was not midnight. It was not raining" (176). The concluding sentences are more than self-contradictory. The last two sentences contradict the first two sentences of Moran's story; they cancel everything Moran has told us. Moreover, with the change from the past to the present tense, they create a new beginning. And, since Moran has learned to speak in the voice of Molloy, he may be beginning what we had considered to be the novel's first section. That is, Molloy may not be the initial storyteller but only a character in a story by Moran.

In *Malone Dies* and *The Unnamable*, each new storyteller resembles his predecessor, except that he is older, less mobile, and more capable of discovering possibilities within ever-narrowing limits. Moreover, each new storyteller denies the independent existence of his predecessor. "I have only to open my mouth for it to testify to the old story, my old story," says Malone. "But let us leave these morbid matters and get on with that of my demise, in two or three days if I remember rightly. Then it will be all over with the Murphys, Merciers, Molloys, Morans, and Malones, unless it goes on beyond the grave" (236). And the Unnamable sees Malone pass before him, although it may be Molloy wearing Malone's hat. But it may also be, says the Unnamable, that "it is I who pass before him" (292-93). And "it is equally possible . . . that I too am in perpetual motion, accompanied by Malone, as the earth by its moon" (295). Indeed, as we move from one novel of the trilogy to the next, we experience perpetual motion and perpetual uncertainty about the narrative center. Our only certainty is of an autonomous narrative voice that usurps each successive narrator, or of the words on the printed page that generate themselves, create each narrator in turn, and ultimately undermine them all.

Malone tells us that, while waiting to die, he will tell stories. He also tells us that "this exercise-book is my life" (274), and we become aware that he is coterminus with his pencil, which is growing shorter and shorter. Malone, therefore, is no more than the product of his diminishing pencil in the exercise book we are reading. And though Molloy seemed to have created new life through his intercourse with the words that filled up his pages, Malone's pencil moves toward the end of death. It creates a whole new cast of characters and brings Malone into existence as their ostensible creator. But Malone also extends the story line by killing off its characters. "How many have I killed, hitting them on the head or setting fire to them?" (236). He kills off Molloy and Moran by placing them in his exercise book, or reducing them from independent narrators to the products of his pencil. He kills off Sapo by changing his name to Macmann. He kills off Moll because he tires of her. He kills off Macmann, Maurice, Ernest, and Lady Pedal by creating a murderer called Lemuel. Malone himself vanishes from the final pages of the exercise book, which is his life, as his pencil runs out of lead. On the last page Lemuel "raises his hatchet on which the blood will never dry, but not to hit anyone, he will not hit anyone, he will not hit anyone any more" (288). And finally Lemuel is no more. There are only the words:

> never anything
> there
> any more

Only the words persist. Malone will be reduced to an obsession of the succeeding narrator, who is himself both the creation and the victim of an autonomous, threatening, and persistent flow of words.

The narrator of *The Unnamable* is alone and immobile. As a stump of life who can no longer feel his limits, he is no more than a point of consciousness. He has no physical locus except within the perpetual movement of the words that issue from him, though

they are not his. With the very end in sight—that is, the blank
space on the final page—he says:

> all words, there's nothing else, you must go on, that's all I know,
> they're going to stop, I know that well, I can feel it, they're going to
> abandon me, it will be the silence, for a moment, a good few moments,
> or it will be mine, the lasting one, that didn't last, that still lasts, it will
> be I, you must go on, I can't go on, you must go on, I'll go on, you must
> say the words, as long as there are any, until they find me, until they
> say me, strange pain, strange sin, you must go on, perhaps it's done
> already, perhaps they have said me already, perhaps they have car-
> ried me to the threshold of my story, before the door that opens on my
> story, that would surprise me, if it opens, it will be I, it will be the
> silence, where I am, I don't know, I'll never know, in the silence you
> don't know, you must go on, I can't go on, I'll go on. (414)

The Unnamable is in perpetual motion, "going nowhere, coming from nowhere"(294). At one point in an unparagraphed rush
of 110 pages, he tries to tell the story of Mahood. But he finds that
it was Mahood who "told me stories about me . . . his voice continued to testify for me, as though woven into mine, preventing me
from saying who I was" (309). In the opening of the trilogy, Molloy
seemed to create a son through the power of grammar—by shifting from the conditional present to the indicative (or actual) past
tense. I say "seemed to" because we have gained perspective on
Molloy. His creative power and independent existence have been
threatened by a succession of narrators, each of whom has reduced his predecessor to the product of his own apparent voice.
Now we realize the power that grammar exercises against the
narrators themselves, for the final narrator is denied his very
existence by a third-person past tense. He cannot say "I am"
because he cannot say "I was." In his trilogy Beckett has not only
brought the narrative voice—the medium's basic element—into
his dramatic compass, he has created a comic-tragic agon between his narrators and that voice which is the very source of
their power and existence. "I trust there is nothing in common,"
says the Unnamable, "between me and that miscreant who
mocked the gods, invented fire, denatured clay and domesticated
the horse, in a word obliged humanity" (303). But he has a great
deal in common with Prometheus—in his defiance, in his attempt
to steal for man the source of power, in his futile but heroic self-
affirmation, and in his perpetual suffering.

In *Ulysses* Joyce discovered the potential of language as an
autonomous, self-generating force. And though he realizes its
threatening potential, his medium attaining the level of a dra-

matic counterforce, he ultimately affirms its creative power. In the final chapter we have more than Molly's monologue. It is the language that transforms her into an earth goddess; language burgeons with an experience of fullness and affirmation, which continues to develop in *Finnegans Wake.* Beckett begins by realizing the creative power of language—and this is his debt to Joyce. But he ends by discovering its full autonomy as a capricious, threatening, and literally self-denying force.

CHAPTER FIVE

Enter the Frame:
The Loss of Clarity

Narrative is distinguished from all other forms of art by the voice of a narrator who intercedes between the subject and the listener or reader. The traditional novel is distinguished by the narrator's view, which the narrative voice describes and which, therefore, also stands between the subject and the reader. The narrator's view follows from his choosing a detached and fixed vantage, even when he narrows his focus to the mind of a central intelligence, and from his enclosing his subject within a convenient frame. Ironically, the narrator's view gains in objectivity and clarity—becomes easier to grasp or hold on to—through a suppression of the frame that he imposes upon his subject, as well as a suppression of the medium through which he fashions his narrative. Pamela's gifts, Allworthy's vista, Yorick's saddle, Gervaise's room, what Stephen sees in the first four chapters of the *Portrait* , all may lack visual vitality. But they are easy to grasp because the narrator, standing on a fixed vantage, orders and frames the details before he recounts them to us. The objects in Vauxhall garden and the young women on the library steps are more vivid because we see them as the narrators see them, their attention aroused and their eyes flashing from point to point. But what we see is still clear because Matthew and Lydia frame what they see within the form of their letters, and Joyce's narrator frames what Stephen sees by remaining, however inobtrusive, between his subject and his reader.

What we experience in the later Joyce, Faulkner, and Beckett derives from a radical change in narrative dynamics. The narrator is no longer situated between his subject and the reader, he no longer stands on a fixed vantage, and he no longer encloses the subject within the frame of his visual imagination. He enters the frame of the narrative. The medium asserts itself as an independent source of interest and control. The narrative voice loses its independent and dominant status. What the reader sees is no longer a clear picture contained within the narrator's purview, but an erratic image where the narrator, the subject, and the medium are brought into the same imaginative field of interaction, an image that is shattered, confused, self-contradictory, but with an independent life of its own.

What the reader of a modernist novel may see is like what the viewer sees in Eisenstein's *Potemkin*, when the crowd flees the advancing soldiers down the Odessa steps: soldiers fragmented into boots and rifles and marching mechanically, people running down endless steps and off in impossible directions, motion sped to a frenzy and slowed unendurably, perspectives maddeningly shifted, shots repeated, lines unnaturally accented, light and shadow in unnatural relation, and in the midst of the terrorized crowd a huge mirror doubling what we see of a student's face as he watches the slaughter around him. It is also like what we all see in a cubist painting, where faces, backs, arms, objects—all on different planes—as well as unnatural colors, obtrusive contours, and surprising textures are all brought onto the same surface. And it is like what we try to see when reading physicists' accounts of elementary particles that are described as *both* continuous waves and discontinuous particles—and which are, as physicists say, "unpicturable." Developments in the modern novel, then, are part of a galaxy of developments that emerge in the twentieth century. What begins, in every field, as an attempt to make us see more sharply, ends with an experience that cannot be held within our visual imagination. To understand these developments, and to establish a base from which we can explain the unpicturable motion in Joyce, Faulkner, and Beckett as well as in Nabokov, Pynchon, Robbe-Grillet, Coover, and the contemporary field of surfiction, we must turn back to an earlier galaxy of developments in the Renaissance.[1]

Hugh Kenner reminds us that the philosophy of Descartes, "which makes the whole of intelligible reality depend on the mental processes of a solitary man," came into being at the same time as the "curious literary form called the novel."[2] The traditional novel's intelligible reality does indeed depend on what the narrator frames in his mind, and the narrator is indeed solitary as he chooses his detached and fixed vantage. Let us, therefore, follow

Kenner's lead and approach the traditional novel through a series of innovations that, like Descartes, helped establish an intellectual and imaginative approach to reality that would dominate Western thought until the twentieth century.

In his *Dialogue of the New Sciences*, Galileo shows how he arrived at the principle of inertia: "I conceive as the work of my own mind a moving object launched above a horizontal plane and freed of all impediment."[3] In a solitary ordeal and a break not only from tradition but from reality, Galileo imagined an ideal picture freed from the impediments that objects naturally encounter; and, as Ortega y Gasset remarks, it was by just this imaginative act that Galileo founded the new science.[4] But Ortega, in seizing on the relationship between science and art, only begins to realize the potential of his subject. It was a particular pattern of imaginative activity and picturing that distinguished Galileo's achievement— a pattern like that which established the new philosophy, the new art, and the new literature. Galileo's pattern can be divided into three stages, although Galileo himself might not have conceived them this way. First, he created an ideal picture; that is, from the detached perspective of a solitary but ideal viewer, he framed his subject or isolated it from the clutter and continuity of its context. Second, he reintroduced the impediments to reconstitute the "full" or "real" picture, implying a relationship between the impediments or a quantity of visible elements and a sense of reality.[5] Third, he transformed his three-dimensional mental picture of a moving object into a two-dimensional and static picture—a series of dots framed by the coordinates of time and space.

Now, Galileo did not invent the system of coordinates, nor did he realize their geometrical potential, and the history of this mathematical construct has two interesting parallels in the history of Western arts and letters. Shortly after the coordinates were invented, in the early fifteenth century, Alberti developed a system of perspective. By looking through a tiny opening in a small box, he found that he could translate the exact proportions of a three-dimensional object into a two-dimensional plane.[6] Alberti established a new art, like Galileo, by imposing a frame upon a cluttered and continuous field from the detached perspective of an ideal viewer, by filling his frame with a quantity of "realistic" detail, and by reducing a three-dimensional and dynamic perception to a static, two-dimensional form.

The second interesting point relating to the development of coordinate geometry came shortly after Galileo used the system to discover the principle of inertia, when Descartes helped develop it into a major scientific tool. Descartes applied the same imaginative pattern in his *Discourse on Method* to establish the new philosophy. Since Descartes doubted the lessons of custom, habit, authority, and the senses, he imposed a frame upon the clutter and continuity of history from the perspective of an ideal, solitary, and detached viewer; his ideal picture, freed from all but the necessary elements, consisted of the fact of his doubting and, hence, of his existence. From this certain fact he reconstituted the "full" or "real" world: the First Cause, the heavens, the stars, the earth, water, air, fire, minerals, and so on. And he arrived at his picture of the world through deductive logic. That is, he reduced and translated a dynamic field into that static language of geometry—a system of points whose relationship, he tells us, could be best understood if viewed as "subsisting between straight lines."[7]

Alberti imposed his frame upon the dynamic field of visual experience, Galileo upon a universe filled with moving objects and impediments, Descartes upon the movement of history. A similar step was taken by Defoe, Richardson, and Fielding (Sterne being the singular exception, who prefigured the course of modernism). Of course, the frame was not invented in the Renaissance, but it did serve a new purpose and carry a new message. In the Middle Ages the frame was an outer edge—a limit to the imaginative construction that called attention to the act of imagination and to the fact of its being shaped in a particular medium. In the Renaissance the frame began to be a limit imposed upon the real world. As the novel developed away from the oral tradition, the narrator gradually shifted his role from that of professional storyteller toward that of witness. He found ways to disguise or suppress the fact that he was conveying a fiction through artificial conventions, and he imposed the frame upon reality itself. Boccaccio, following in the specific tradition of the fourteenth-century *favellatore* and in the general tradition of storytellers from the epic to the *fabliaux*, was retelling stories with eloquence and evocative power. His "Preface to the Ladies" called attention to itself as a frame that enclosed his stories. Chaucer created a narrator who claims to have witnessed the events of his narrative; but his pretense is an obvious convention, and his frame is seen only as a more skillfully created device than Boccaccio's. What distinguishes the traditional novel from the epic, the early short narrative, and the stories told within the walled garden of a plagued city or the time encompassed by a journey to Canterbury is our sense of the narrator not as a storyteller but as a witness who has imposed his frame upon reality. Whether his story is told in the first or third person, the narrator is present as a witness who holds a world of time and space within his solitary purview.

Indeed, the narrator of the novel, with his detached and fixed viewpoint and his enclosing frame, is very much like the ideal intellect that was postulated by Laplace at the end of the eighteenth century that would serve as a scientific model for the next hundred years. This "intellect which at a given instant knew all the forces acting in nature, and the position of all things of which the world consists . . . would embrace in the same formula the motions of the greatest bodies in the universe and those of the slightest atoms; nothing would be uncertain for it, and the future, like the past, would be present to its eyes."[8]

In the Renaissance a stance was developed to view objects defined not by their inherent qualities, limits, or dynamics but by their relation to a fixed observer governing a closed system. The term "realistic"—deriving from the Latin *res*, or "thing"—aptly applies to this kind of objectification. It applies, that is, to Galileo's ideal picture, which he transformed to a coordinate graph; to the view through Alberti's little box, which he transformed onto a two-dimensional canvas; to the world picture generated by the solitary mind of Descartes, which he structured on the principles of geometry. And to the purview of the narrative persona who imposes his frame on a continuous stream of events, holds the movement of the past, present, and future before him, and fits the dynamic details of character, setting, commentary, motivation, and action into the static grid of his plot.

It is the frame that gives the narrator's picture its peculiar clarity—a clarity, for all the novel's illusion of movement through time, that is essentially geometrical. And yet in order to evoke an illusion of objective reality, the frame, as an idealized or esthetic limit, was suppressed. The frame would seem to say, "The world of space and time outside of me is qualitatively the same but is unnecessary and would blur my focus. Moreover, you should forget that only *some* of the visual details (not every blade of grass) and only some moments in the sequence of time (not every word or action) are actually included within me." As realism in the arts and sciences developed, more and more details were included within the frame and more skill was manifested in their representation—and the message was always that the creation was real, full, and complete.

The picture's clarity was also achieved through a suppression of medium: the canvas as a two-dimensional object, the stage as a framework for carefully plotted and skillfully executed action, and the novel as an artfully contrived sequence of words virtually disappeared. The two-dimensional canvas would seem to say, "I am three-dimensional reality." The proscenium stage would seem to say, "I am a real room with the fourth wall removed." The novel would seem to say, "I am really happening."

Now let us examine the evolution of the narrative stance paradigmatically by focusing on four works where the story-frame plays and important role: Henry James's *The Turn of the Screw*, an apparently simple illustration of traditional fiction reaching for a sophisticated extreme of objectivity; Joseph Conrad's *Heart of Darkness*, where the story as story asserts itself as the true subject; William Faulkner's *Absalom, Absalom!*, where the story as main subject is beyond the grasp of the storytellers and the reader; and Samuel Beckett's trilogy, where the central conflict becomes that between the storytellers and the story—indeed, between the storyteller and the storytelling voice—or between various formal elements of the fiction itself.

Henry James's novella *The Turn of the Screw* is a useful illustration of traditional fiction reaching a limit, not only because it is short but because one of its chief aims is to bring an ostensibly fantastic story within the grasp of realistic objectivity. The narrative structure begins with the frame of a detached and fixed narrator, who underscores his detachment by remaining nameless. Within his frame is the frame of Douglas, who is telling a story to the guests of the manor. Douglas is not so detached from the story, for he had been involved with the protagonist for twenty years in a way that he can only intimate, and he has preserved this relationship in his memory for the twenty years since she died. Within Douglas's frame is the frame of the governess, this time not the voice of a living character telling a story from memory but the manuscript of a woman long since dead, who, as the style suggests, composed a traumatic experience into an extremely controlled story. Hence the real subject, contained within her frame, is absolutely beyond our grasp. This does not mean that the ultimate picture is unclear. Quite the contrary. We see the frame imposed by each narrator and the story contained within these frames with absolute clarity. It is only the subject, what actually happened, that remains beyond our final grasp. The story is not unclear but ambiguous. Our perception is like that of the viewer who tries to fix on the ambiguous picture, common to psychology, that E. H. Gombrich discusses in *Art and Illusion*[9] (see below). When we read *The Turn of the Screw*, we may see Peter Quint as a demonic ghost or as a figment of a repressed imagination, just as we can see either a rabbit or a duck in the drawing. We may shift from one to the other, but, as Gombrich points out, we can never see both at once. The images may be contradictory, but no single perception contains a self-contradiction.

Joseph Conrad's *Heart of Darkness* is also structured on the principle of a frame within a frame, but the narrative stance and dynamics are entirely different. Again the largest frame is provided by an unnamed narrator. He is not so detached as the first narrator in James's novella, for, as a comparison of his opening and closing descriptions shows, the story has a profound effect on his consciousness. Nonetheless, he imposes his frame from a detached and fixed vantage. Within his frame sits Marlow, in the lotus-flower position, who tells the main story. But Marlow's stories are not like those of the typical seaman—or those of the traditional narrator, including the narrators of *The Turn of the Screw*—"the whole meaning of which lies within the shell of a cracked nut."[10] For Marlow "the meaning of an episode was not inside like a kernel but outside, enveloping the tale which brought it out." The subject of the *Heart of Darkness* is not a series of events contained within a frame but Marlow's story as story, a dynamic process where style, description, characters, symbols, actions are constantly evolving—and where all these elements are brought into the same dynamic field of imaginative perception and meaning. Conrad does not, cannot, focus on the heart of darkness: the landscape was "great, expectant, mute. . . . I felt how big, how confoundedly big, was that thing that couldn't talk, and perhaps was deaf as well. . . . Somehow it didn't bring any image with it" (94). Nor can he focus on Kurtz, or hold onto a complete image of him: "The man presented himself as a voice" (119). And when, near the very end of the story, he is finally brought onto the scene, all we see is "the thin arm extended commandingly, the lower jaw moving, the eyes of that apparition shining darkly far in its boney head" (135).

Conrad does not try to focus on the heart of darkness, on Kurtz—on the kernel of his story or a static subject within the shell of a frame—but on the "enveloping" and developing tale, the *movement* of Marlow's story. He does, however, frame Marlow's tale and provide a stable vantage for the reader. The first narrator, despite the changed perspective that results from his vicarious experience, does stand between the reader and Marlow. He does recount his own story from a fixed point in time and space. He does enclose his subject—Marlow telling his story—within a traditional frame.

Faulkner's *Absalom, Absalom!* aims directly at the kernel, or the character of Thomas Sutpen, whose story would seem to provide the meaning of Western history—from its sources in classical and biblical times to those of frontier American and the antebellum South—and to provide the link between the past and the present. But the kernel is never grasped or directly encountered, for it is approached from the vantage of four characters with different preconceptions, needs, obsessions, and degrees of relationship to Sutpen. Rosa—the one character who ever saw Sutpen, and the object of his traumatic insult—is dominated by puritanic repressions and a Gothic imagination. "Out of a quiet thunderclap," she sees him "abrupt (man-horse-demon) upon a scene peaceful and decorous as a school prize watercolor."[11] Mr. Compson, having heard a great deal of the story from his father, an apparently reliable witness, has stoically come to terms with the outrages of history. For him Sutpen seems to have been "created out of thin air and set down in the bright summer sabbath sunshine in the middle of a tired foxtrot" (32). Quentin—obsessed by chivalric values and love for his sister, ambivalent about a history where the sources of affirmation and negation are one—focuses less on Sutpen than on his son and daughter. And Shreve—detached from the situation historically, emotionally, and psychologically, but genuinely curious and imaginatively sympathetic—focuses more on Sutpen's nobel bastard son.

What we see in our experience of *Absalom, Absalom!* is not a clear or even an ambiguous picture of Sutpen or the events of his legend, and though the novel leads us to reconstruct the events and fit the pieces of the picture puzzle together, to end at this point is to deny the primary experience of the novel. For the legend of Sutpen is beyond our imaginative perception, owing to the psychological and historical limitations of each narrator. Indeed, the gaps between each narrator and the central story assert themselves as a dramatic part of the novel's fabric. Nor, as in *The Turn of the Screw*, do we see a series of frames, one within the other. What we see are four partially overlapping and constantly shifting frames attempting to enclose a subject that is not there. The subject of the novel is not an enveloping or developing story but a kinetic montage of storytellers as they try to impose a frame and reconstitute the "full" or "real" picture.

As in *Heart of Darkness*, various elements of subject and medium are brought into the same field of perception and meaning, but they are not enclosed within the frame of a solitary, fixed, and detached narrator. There is a narrative voice that encompasses the four narrating characters; but it does not frame them, for it is not fixed in time or space, nor is it detached or always separable from the characters. While it creates a syntactical distance and continuity by turning each "I" into a "he" or a "she," it also insinuates itself into the voice and view of each narrating character—sometimes unobtrusively as subtext, sometimes breaking through with its own allusions, images, rhythms, and intensities. It is the voice of a hovering narrator who does not provide a frame but, like the narrating characters, tries to apprehend an experience that remains unclear and beyond his grasp. Moreover, it is responsible for the shifting of frames and caesurae—as it shifts its stance from one of identification to one of intrusion or usurpation, as it shifts its focus from one narrating character to another, as it shifts its perspective to bring us into the presence of different narrators simultaneously. In *Absalom, Absalom!* the frames that attempt to enclose the subject and the dynamic of shifting frames are experienced as part of the subject.

What we have seen so far in this paradigmatic development from traditional to modern fiction is that, as the narrator relinquishes his detached stance and eliminates the distance from his subject, he can no longer enclose the subject and keep it fixed within a frame; and the medium, less amenable to his control, asserts itself as an independent and dynamic part of the subject. Therefore, the narrator's view loses its clarity, and we can no longer hold on to what we see in our visual imagination. In Samuel Beckett's trilogy, as we have seen, not only the view but the very voice of the narrator is called into question, and the medium not only liberates itself from the narrator's control but threatens to deny him his very existence.

In the trilogy, as in *Absalom, Absalom!*, we encounter a montage of shifting frames, which finally draws us into the Unnamable's experience of perpetual motion. But in *Absalom, Absalom!* there is a primary narrator, and—although he enters the frame of the narrative, shifts his focus from one narrating character to the next, and hovers near each of them to create a palpable uncertainty—he retains his narrative identity. In Beckett's trilogy one narrator yields to the next, and we become increasingly uncertain about the narrative source. That the final narrator is unnamable establishes our ultimate uncertainty. A key word in the trilogy is *aporia*, the rhetorical device of doubting. But unlike Descartes's the Unnamable's doubting cannot lead to the affirmation of a doubter, and hence of his existence, for the Unnamable goes so far as to doubt the very voice with which he doubts. The narrative voice in Beckett's trilogy is not only inseparable from the subject but is the major antagonist. At once liberated from its traditional position between the subject and the reader and gratuitously imposing itself upon the narrator, it threatens to usurp the narrator-protagonist while continually undermining the narrative view.

Hugh Kenner has shown how Beckett extends and parodies the line of Descartes, who, like the classical novelist, "made the whole of reality depend on the mental processes of a solitary man." We might go further, to say that Beckett stretches the line to its breaking point—and destroys not only the Cartesian enterprise and the strategy that gave rise to classical physics, perspective painting, and the novel, but the very essence of narrative. It is indeed the achievement of Beckett's anti-narrative to evoke a vital protagonist even though the very sources of fictional characterization— the narrator's voice and narrator's view—are denied. He realizes what would seem to be an impossibility by creating a comic-tragic conflict between his narrator and the narrative voice, or between his protagonist and the limits of his medium—which results in perpetual suffering, perpetual affirmation, perpetual negation, and perpetual motion.

CHAPTER SIX

Dislocation in Nabokov's
Black (Hole) Humor: *Lolita* and *Pale Fire*

The novel in motion, then, begins with the urge to see; it causes us to see even the most static scene more vividly than the traditional novel, through a series of visual dislocations. As the novel in motion develops, the dislocations become more disorienting. The narrator changes his point of view more swiftly and radically. Then he changes his stance: he no longer stands between us and what happened but enters the frame of the novel. He relinquishes his privileged position and becomes one of the fictional elements, like the characters. The act of narration becomes part of the subject, part of what has happened—or, since it is no longer intermediate, part of what is happening. When the narrator relinquishes his intermediate position and stable vantage, we no longer have a frame to contain what we see. We do not encounter an experience held within the frame of the narrator's purview, but rather a field of elements whose relations are constantly changing. We experience continual displacement and dislocation; we are constantly dislodged and disrupted. What we see in our visual imagination, though vivid, is impossible to grasp or contain.

Disruption is a break in continuity. Displacement results in the absence of place, dislocation the absence of location. As the novel in motion develops, the break becomes more prominent and the absence is encountered as a dramatic presence—or, as Eisenstein calls it, a caesura. Indeed, our experience of motion is the result of narrative gaps, missing links, and empty spaces in the text. Of course, movement requires space, as we know by recalling Zeno's ingenious but unpersuasive argument. Playing with Parmenides' conceptual view as if it were reality, Zeno argued that because there was an infinite number of points—and therefore no empty spaces between them—there could be no movement. The arrow could never reach its destination because it always had to pass through one more point. It could move no distance at all because a point could always be postulated before the next one. That is, there could be no movement because all of space was full. But the arrow does move. There is space for it to travel through. And, we might conclude from Zeno's failure, the more space, the more room for movement.

The classical view of physical reality that developed in the Renaissance and eighteenth century and held sway until modern times certainly included the fact that things moved through space. But space was not literally empty, and movement obeyed regular laws. Laplace's ideal intellect would behold no real gaps, no quantum jumps, no uncertainty. And it is interesting that the traditional narrator, like Laplace's ideal intellect, both frames his picture and implicitly fills up all the space. Of course, he does not describe every detail of Allworthy's vista or Gervaise's room, nor does he account for every moment in a character's life. But he fills in enough of his narrative picture to imply that it is full.[1] And as the novelist becomes more concerned with verisimilitude, the narrator provides a greater quantity of details—hence the effect of Joyce's parody in the "Ithaca" chapter of *Ulysses*. Indeed, we criticize the traditional novel if it fails to account for an item that should be there, if the story has a missing link, if it omits a crucial scene, if a character who has engaged our interest suddenly disappears.

In *Portrait of the Artist*, Joyce cuts sharply from Stephen's childhood, when he hides under the table in fear of the eagle pulling out his eyes, to his youth in the Clongowes playing field, and then from the sterile infirmary to the warm fire banked high and red beneath the ivy branches. But he fills in the space between each section with a series of asterisks—which imply continuity and stand for the moments he left out. In *Ulysses* he disrupts the continuity and dislocates the reader by omitting the asterisks. We feel the jolt when, having just settled into the world of the Martello tower, we suddenly find ourselves in a schoolroom, hearing a teacher we do not yet know is Stephen question his students. And we are startled when, having just read a meticulous account of what Bloom says and does not say to Molly before going to sleep, we suddenly discover that we missed his request for breakfast in bed. Joyce shares with Eisenstein an instinct for the jump-cut.

The narrative gaps and empty spaces in Joyce, Faulkner, and

Beckett are dynamic elements in the medium that the reader directly encounters and that directly cause palpable disruptions. In Joyce they enhance the effect of the medium as a gratuitous force. In Faulkner they prevent the narrator and reader from grasping a senseless experience. In Beckett they intrude to undermine the possibility of knowing even what is most elemental and necessary. To Vladimir Nabokov they are the source of creative destruction—which, on the one hand, looks back to the ancient tradition of diabolic comedy and, on the other, looks forward to breakthroughs in modern physics and modern fiction.

In a filmed interview Nabokov describes "the first thrill of diabolical pleasure you have in discovering that you have somehow cheated creation by creating something yourself."[2] The thrill is diabolic, first, because his creation is independent of prior creation, defiant of ultimate "reality," and in its own blasphemous way *ex nihilo*, or "out of nothing." The thrill is also diabolic because the cheating entails an annihilation of prior creation—a canny dismantling or gleeful decimation of the everyday world, everyday fantasies, and everyday literary conventions. Nabokov's "thrill of diabolical pleasure" is like the thrill that animated the Roman Saturnalia and that found its medieval expression in the Feast of Fools, the miracle plays, and the *sotie* drama. By reflecting on three points in the medieval development of diabolic comedy, we may gain a perspective on Nabokov's achievement.[3]

The Feast of Fools was an English New Year's revel that loosened traditional restraints, allowing the release of a joyful demonic energy. To use a medieval trope, "the world was turned upside down": priests and clerks wore monstrous masks, ate blood puddings during mass, played dice on the altar, leaped through the church, drove through town in shabby carts regaling everyone with "infamous performances . . . indecent gestures and verses scurrilous and unchaste."[4]

In the English miracle plays, the diabolic comic impulse became more formalized; and as the energy became more controlled and more comic, it became more threatening. Pilate amused the spectators by toying with his wife before calling Jesus before him; devilish tormentors would blindfold Christ and make Him guess who scourged Him last, or make a farce out of fitting His body onto a cross that had been carelessly made the wrong size. The devils and tormentors were energetic, inventive, comic, skillful, and successful. By "turning their work into sport," they presented "Hell to their victims as an unending, varied game." In their malicious play they achieved an experience of evil—the destruction of divine order. And yet they also succeeded in bringing the biblical drama to life.[5]

In France, which did not tolerate fools in its church or clowning with its liturgy, the diabolic comic impulse was secularized in year-round fool societies and formalized in their *sotie* drama. The fools in these plays were as skillful in their acrobatics as they were with their verbal wit. Turning handsprings in the midst of their satiric banter, they would gleefully defy the laws of gravity and grammar as well as social convention. In the end a comic free-for-all would bring a "jerry-built new world tumbling about their ears."[6] The *sotie* fools, that is, realized their vitality and exercised their mental and physical skills in the total destruction of the ordinary world.

In the Feast of Fools, the miracle plays, and the *sotie* drama, creative vitality is achieved through the playful release of destructive energy, the diabolic thrill of turning life into a game, the comic urge toward disorder and nihilistic destruction. In the end order gives way to a senseless motion, the world is turned upside down, stable reality is undermined by a comic force that is at once threatening and enlivening. And, as the force becomes more threatening and enlivening, its manipulators become more skillful and daring. The diabolic thrill, then, comes from the exercise of skills that demolish social and psychological orders, leaving only the game or the act—the arbitrary and precarious movement that evinces skillful control and creative daring, and that destroys our security while awakening our senses, our feelings, and our intellects.

One of the most vivid modern realizations of the impulse I have been trying to define is in Nabokov's *Ada*—in the extraordinary act that Van Veen performed in the guise of Mascodagama. It began with an empty stage, when, "after five heartbeats of theatrical suspense, something swept out of the wings, enormous and black . . . a shapeless nastiness," which precipitated in the audience "something similar to the 'primordial qualm' ":

> Into the harsh light of its gaudily carpeted space a masked giant, fully eight feet tall, erupted, running strongly in the kind of soft boots worn by Cossack dancers. A voluminous, black shaggy cloak of the *burka* type enveloped his *silhouette inquiétante* . . . from neck to knee or what appeared to be those sections of his body. A Karakul cap surmounted his top. A black mask covered the upper part of his heavily bearded face. The unpleasant colossus kept strutting up and down the stage for a while, then the strut changed to the restless walk of a caged

madman, then he whirled, and to a clash of cymbals in the orchestra and a cry of terror (perhaps faked) in the gallery, Mascodagama turned over in the air and stood on his head.

In this weird position, with his cap acting as a pseudopodal pad, he jumped up and down, pogo-stick fashion—and suddenly came apart. Van's face, shining with sweat, grinned between the legs of the boots that still shod his rigidly raised arms. Simultaneously his real feet kicked off and away the false head with its crumpled cap and bearded mask. The magic reversal "made the house gasp."[7]

The "magic reversal" is more than the discovery of Van right-side up when we thought him upside down. It is a reversal that destroys our equilibrium, our sense of which way is up, our normal frame of reference, our stable sense of "reality." Mascodagama upright—ugly, massive, erratic, masking upside down Van—is threatening. Van upside down—bouncing on his hands like a pogo stick, playing the upright giant—is comic. Mascodagama coming apart is frightening. Van kicking away Mascodagama's fake head is comic—but he is also frightening because at this point we recognize the union of the strange colossus and the familiar Van, of the erratic and the controlled, of the menacing and the impish. When the mask and costume and performance have been recognized for what they are, all our links with "reality" have been destroyed: all that remains is a flat stage and Van's shining face and diabolic grin, and even this reality is undermined by the narrator's ironic style. The narrator, who has no place within the world of the novel, has told us that only "the work of a poet" could describe Van's extraordinary act (especially a poet of the "Black Belfry group" [183]). The ultimate diabolic act, then, is the work of the narrator-poet: the work itself, the verbal surface—which is like a stage whose wings do not open to an outside world. Or a mask that only masks another mask worn by an actor cavorting over a black hole, fully aware of the danger but taking joy in the fact that he has made the hole and his precarious act.

Nabokov's strategy is to create a recognizable world and then through a series of dislocations undermine, deconstruct, annihilate every possible vantage from which we might form judgments. In the end he leaves us with a rich, engaging, and continually shifting verbal surface suspended, as it were, above a black hole. His singular achievement, then, might be called black-hole humor. This critical metaphor leads from the diabolic tradition to the tradition of modernism, which develops the potential of discontinuity, dislocation, and displacement, as well as the imaginative defiance of modern astronomers who first postulated and

then discovered a "black hole" in space. I will apply it to two of
Nabokov's important and interestingly related novels: *Lolita*,
where we are cunningly led along the shifting surface, continually dislocated and trapped in its discontinuities by a narrator
who is always beyond our grasp; and *Pale Fire*, where we encounter a black hole that is not figurative but literal and
physical—and that may have led Robbe-Grillet, another master of
discontinuity and physical space in the text, to say that this book
"comes very close to expressing my feelings."[8]

Lolita (1955) was Nabokov's twelfth novel, the third written in
English after his departure from Europe in 1940. "It had taken me
some forty years to invent Russia and Western Europe," he tells us
in his epilogue, "now I was faced by the task of inventing America."[9] What Nabokov invented was the drive—and aimless driving or movement—toward some evanescent goal, which had obsessed American novelists from Fitzgerald to Kerouac; the speech
and manners of an adolescent girl, which few American writers
had even looked at; the American motelscape, just before it gave
way to the superhighways; the drugstore, before its soda fountain
was replaced by the dirty-book rack (which the paperback indus-
try created for the likes of *Lolita*); the department store, with its
"touch of the mythological and the enchanted" (100); the bohe-
mian suburban housewife; the progressive girls' school. Much of
Lolita is like *Sister Carrie* or *An American Tragedy*, where
Dreiser deliberately recorded details of those American institutions he knew would become historical. Thus, the Haze house is a
"white-frame horror . . . looking dingy and old, more gray than
white—the kind of place you know will have a rubber tube af-
fixable to the tub faucet in lieu of shower" (36). And Humbert jots
down his early recollections "on the leaves of what is commer-
cially known as a 'typewriter tablet' " (40). But the realistic details
in *Lolita* are magnified and at times singularly distorted by the
lens of Humbert Humbert's language, which is the product of a
foreign consciousness. A row of parked cars are "like pigs at a
trough" (108). A fire hydrant is seen as "a hideous thing, really,
painted a thick silver and red, extending the red stumps of its
arms to be varnished by the rain which like stylized blood dripped
upon its argent chains. No wonder that stopping beside those
nightmare cripples is taboo" (98–99). The reader of *Lolita*, then, is
constantly dislocated by the shifts and gaps between the familiar
and the strange.

Humbert Humbert's foreign consciousness is due to more than

his European upbringing and his perverse sensibilities. He is made foreign, and removed from our reach, by the "bizarre cognomen . . . his own invention . . . this mask—through which two hypnotic eyes seem to glow" (6). He is removed, that is, by the persona, created by a narrator whose real identity and ultimate purpose are slyly kept beyond our reach. And he is doubly removed, from the outset of the novel, by being such a persona in a memoir edited by the improbable John Ray, Jr., Ph.D., who has been awarded the Poling Prize for a "modest" work, "Do the Senses make Sense?" (5). Indeed, the foreword, being a parody of that device used to establish verisimilitude ever since *The Scarlet Letter*, destroys any bridge between the world of the novel and the world where the daily papers are supposed to have carried references to Humbert's crime.

The novel proper is cast as a memoir, a form usually written in a style of sincerity if not modesty, and usually designed to reveal the personality of its author and the tenor of his time through a coherent sequence of selected events and ponderings. It is also cast in the form of another traditional sequence and pattern of purposeful motion: the quest. Humbert's singular quest has two models, which are also kinds of memoirs. The first is Dante's: from the inspiration of his nymphet Beatrice to the beatific vision, which Humbert encounters as "the melody of children at play, nothing but that, and so limpid was the air that within this vapor of blended voices, majestic and minute, remote and magically near, frank and divinely enigmatic—one could hear now and then, as if released, an almost articulate spurt of vivid laughter, or the crack of a bat, or the clatter of a toy wagon" (280). The second quest model is Melville's *Moby-Dick*. If on first thought Humbert's nymphet (especially as she is likened to a butterfly) makes an improbable white whale, and the Humbert-Quilty double is a far cry from Ishmael-Ahab, ponder a layer lower, reader—at least upon Humbert's historical, anthropological, and scientific digressions, which realistically ground and epically magnify the proportions of his nymphet and his quest. These forms are not copied, though, but parodied—turning purposeful into purposeless movement, destroying the protagonist's coherence, and undermining our normal expectations, perceptions, and conclusions.

The novel's underlying metaphor also contributes to the pattern of the quest, and, as it is handled, to the dynamic of annihilation. Diana Butler has pointed out the relationship between Humbert's passion for nymphets and Nabokov's own passion for butterflies;[10] indeed, Lolita's peculiar attraction, Humbert's thrills of discovery, and his pangs of horror and guilt are all evoked through the implicit and pervasive metaphor of Lolita as prize butterfly. Moreover, Alfred Appel, Jr., has described how metamorphosis, which characterizes both the butterfly and the nymphet, also characterizes the form of the novel: the development of Lolita from a girl into a woman, Humbert's lust into love, and a crime into a redeeming work of art, so that in the end, "the reader has watched the chrysalis come to life."[11]

But to see the beautiful butterfly at the end of the multiple transformations should not obscure the stages of destruction, or the dislocations, in the process. Humbert Humbert acknowledges: "I knew I had fallen in love with Lolita forever; but I also knew she would not be forever Lolita. She would be thirteen on January 1. In two years or so she would cease being a nymphet and would turn into a 'young girl,' and then, into a 'college girl'—that horror of horrors" (62). Lolita is as changeable and transient as a butterfly, and the narrator's accomplishment is not in capturing but evoking her in an equally changeable and transitory form—a form composed of perspectives that are successively and gleefully destroyed. The kinetic pattern of destruction may be analyzed into two contradictory planes, which we might call endless multiplication and continual forward movement.

In *Lolita*'s opening paragraphs we are given a fine example of Nabokov's style:

> Lolita, light of my life, fire of my loins. My sin, my soul. Lo-lee-ta: the tip of the tongue taking a trip of three steps down the palate to tap, at three, on the teeth. Lo. Lee. Ta.
> She was Lo, plain Lo, in the morning, standing four feet ten in one sock. She was Lola in slacks. She was Dolly at school. She was Dolores on the dotted line. But in my arms she was always Lolita. (11)

The style is perhaps best characterized by its repetitive variation, its ability—through rhythm, sound patterns, puns, precision—to cause us to see an image in multiple flashes. The multiplicity is increased by relating Lolita to Humbert's first love, Annabel, and to the innumerable nymphets in literary history. It is increased even more by the innumerable variations of the same scene of lovestruck Humbert courting the tough-minded and tough-hearted Lolita. The four-page catalog of "Sunset Motels, U-Beam Cottages, Hillcrest Courts, Pine View Courts, Mountain View Courts, Skyline Courts, Park Plaza Courts, Green Acres, Mac's Courts" (134) is one of the most incisive evocations of the American landscape in the 1950s. It is also a dramatic means to convey the multiple and identical scenes that took place during the period of a year and over the expanse of three thousand miles.

Still another way that Nabokov effects an experience of multiplication is through the device of the double. Nabokov may be indebted to Stevenson, Poe, Gogol, and Dostoevsky; but he does not follow them in using the double to explore psychic dimensions of a main character's personality. Claire Quilty, the writer, the man of the stage, the debauchee, the driver of an Aztec-red convertible, is not a projection of the hero: there is no need for a projection in Humbert's full confession. Clare Quilty is a parody and a comic repetition of Humbert Humbert. He mocks the hero, he arouses fresh sympathy for the hero—and he also conveys the impression that Humbert is not unique but one of many. The world is full of nymphets, and nympholepts as well.

The result of Nabokov's tricks of style, structure, and characterization is that we are led through a series of freshly evoked and quickly shattered experiences, which are nearly identical and which take place in a world of nearly identical backdrops. Nabokov destroys our preconceptions of time and space. As we think back, we almost feel as if time were composed of the same moment being repeated over and over, and as if space were pieced together from identical motelscapes.

This is not a complete description of our response though, for the novel also depends on its continuing forward movement through both time and space. We are fascinated by Nabokov's "verbal diddle,"[12] we are affected by the multiplicity, we become lost in the intricate labyrinths, we are led on by the style, which, as Nabokov says of Gogol, follows "the dream road of his superhuman imagination"[13]—but our most immediate concern is what happens next to Humbert Humbert. Will Humbert make contact with Lolita? How will he take care of Charlotte? What will happen when he arrives at Lolita's camp? When will he seduce his nymphet? Will he get caught by the police? Will the red convertible catch up? Will he find his runaway love? Will he get Quilty? If the first main dimension of the novel's structure is endless multiplication, the second is continual forward movement. The multiplication works at cross-purposes to the forward movement but does not impede it. Rather, it creates an eccentric rhythm very much like that which Nabokov attributes to Gogol's "Overcoat": "a combination of two movements: a jerk and a glide. Imagine a trapdoor that opens under your feet with absurd suddenness, and a lyrical gust that sweeps you up and then lets you fall with a bump into the next traphole."[14]

Nabokov's eccentric rhythm achieves its climax in the meeting of the doubles. This obligatory scene is demanded by the novel's continuing forward movement, and yet, after the scene with Dolly Schiller that eliminates Humbert's motivation, it is wholly gratuitous. Humbert fires into the thick pink rug. Quilty continues his banter until, in the midst of a banal question, he throws himself on the avenging gunman. "We rolled all over the floor, in each other's arms, like two huge helpless children. He was naked and goatish under his robe, and I felt suffocated as he rolled over me. I rolled over him. We rolled over me. They rolled over him. We rolled over us." Humbert's second shot sends Quilty into the music room, his fingers wiggling in the air, his rump heaving rapidly, where after a struggle over the door he sits down at the piano and plays "several atrociously vigorous fundamentally hysterical, plangent chords, his jowls quivering, his spread hands tensely plunging, and his nostrils emitting the soundtrack snorts which had been absent from our fight." Struck in the side by Humbert's third bullet, Quilty rises from his chair "higher and higher, like old, gray, mad Nijinski, like Old Faithful . . . head thrown back in a howl, hand pressed to his brow, and with his other hand clutching his armpit as if stung by a hornet." Humbert chases him down the hall "with a kind of double, triple, kangaroo jump . . . bouncing up twice in his wake, and then bouncing between him and the front door in a ballet-like bounce." "Suddenly dignified, and somewhat morose," Clare begins to ascend the broad stairs:

> I fired three or four times in quick succession, wounding him at every blaze; and every time I did it to him, that horrible thing to him, his face would twitch in an absurd clownish manner, as if he were exaggerating the pain . . . [and] he would say under his breath, with a phoney British accent—all the while dreadfully twitching, shivering, smirking, but withal talking in a curiously detached and even amiable manner: "Ah, that hurts, sir, enough! Ah, that hurts atrociously, my dear fellow. I pray you, desist!"

But the chase continues from room to room until Humbert corners the "blood-spattered but still buoyant" Quilty in his bed and shoots him through the blanket at close range: "a big pink bubble with juvenile connotations formed on his lips, grew to the size of a toy balloon, and vanished" (271–78).

We have been swept up and let fall with a bump into the final trap hole. This scene, which is the climax of the novel, coming just a few pages before the end, momentarily destroys our recollection of Humbert's evocations of the nymphet, the delights of his tentative conquests, the perceptions of her special grace, the poignancy of his meeting with Dolly Schiller. After Humbert's total acceptance of Lolita's metamorphosis, there is no explaining his need for vengeance or the slapstick treatment of the gruesome scene. The violent shift in perspective completely destroys the already shifting foundations of the novel; it causes us to doubt the confusing impressions of the narrator that we have built up, as it were, from scratch. What are we to make of a world where perversity is the only form that love can take, where the grotesque is the only form of beauty, where madness is the only form of sanity, where obsession is the only form of freedom, where destruction is the only form of living? What are we to make of Humbert Humbert, the hero, the victim, the creator of this world? Is he the comic-pathetic romantic, forever in search of the unattainable? Is he the true and tender lover of Lolita and Dolly Schiller? Is he the mad sadist, the avenger-killer of Clare Quilty?

The final diabolic shift in perspective forces us to question not Humbert Humbert's grasp of reality but our own. Quilty dies, Dolly dies, Humbert dies. But the narrator, who has gleefully destroyed everything in sight—like the medieval devils and fools, Dostoyevsky's double, and Melville's confidence man—continues to haunt us.

Shifting perspectives are common in modern literature. What distinguishes *Lolita* is the narrator's diabolically comic strategy and stance—or his black-hole humor. The narrator's strategy is black in its ontological defiance and gratuitous but creative annihilation that evoke the "thrill of diabolical pleasure." It is comic in its satiric range and sheer playfulness. And it is marked by the trap holes in its narrative continuum that trip us and cause us to shift perspectives, that take us by surprise and destroy our equillibrium, that undermine our bases for psychological and moral judgment.

The narrator's stance—how and where the narrator stands in relation to his story—also effects a kind of diabolic comedy marked by what we might call a black hole. This is not the trap into which the reader is swept, but the encounter of absence. Indeed, that encounter of absence—or the dramatic presence of absence—is like the encounter of a "black hole" in space, which is caused by a star so massive that its field of gravity has collapsed it to virtually nothing. The narrator of *Lolita* is continually present in the novel. He engages us with his verbal wit, comic destructiveness, and diabolic control. He leads us through an evanescent, undermined, but nonetheless positive experience of longing and love. He is all the while before us—but has cunningly kept himself beyond our reach by his "bizarre cognomen," his subjugation to the improbable John Ray, Jr., and his creation of a persona who changes continually and discontinuously.

In *Pale Fire*[15] we encounter a hole that is not metaphoric but literal and physical. This is the empty space—the blank pages—between the poem "Pale Fire," presumably written by John Shade, and the commentary, presumably written by Charles Kinbote. On one side of the hole are 999 lines of heroic couplets that focus on the poet's love for his wife, the catastrophe of his daughter's possible suicide, and his experience of death and rebirth. On the other side of the hole is a set of notes six times as long as the poem, illuminating those allusions that Shade's wife ("the domestic censor") convinced the poet to suppress or disguise: the "glorious friendship" between Shade and Kinbote and the story of Charles the Beloved, king of Zembla, who was forced to escape his homeland and take up a post incognito at Wordsmith College, where he lived in constant fear of the assassin who started from Zembla on the day when Shade's poem was begun.

The hole in the text opens the question of relationships while, at the same time, obviating any answer. It precludes any certainty about the relationship between the poem and the story that was supposed to inspire it, between Shade and Kinbote, between Charles Kinbote and Charles the Beloved, between Wordsmith College in America and the kingdom of Zembla, between Kinbote (whose name in Zemblan means "regicide") and Gradus (the would-be regicide), between Jakob Gradus and Jack Gray (whom Kinbote confuses with Gradus and who accidentally kills Shade while aiming at Kinbote, whom he has mistaken for the judge who sentenced him to the Institute for the Criminal Insane).

Let us begin with the empty space as a simple physical presence—intrusion. The hole between the poem and commentary opens a rudimentary physical problem: which way does the book go? Should we, with customary respect for the poetic text and our linear habit of mind, read the poem first and then the commentary? Should we follow the editor's advice to read the commentary first and then the poem—along with the notes? Or should we start with the poem and turn to the notes as the spirit moves us? Whichever choice we make, we will continually return to an experience of the book as a physical object divided in two parts, and we will inevitably find ourselves reading in two directions. The empty space divides the poem absolutely from the commentary and compels us to turn back and forth between them. Moreover, as each note grows longer—let's be frank about it—we forget the word or line being annotated, not to mention the stanza or context. We may find ourselves reading the poem backward, or up the page, until we discover where the unit of meaning begins. Certainly, though, we begin to wonder about the actual subject or center: is it Shade the poet, or Kinbote the commentator? We discover that the book is designed to frustrate our sense of center—or that the only center we can know is the empty space that secures our forefinger as we flip between poem and commentary.

Actually, there are three holes in *Pale Fire*: the first between the foreword (which, in the scholarly tradition, describes the manuscript) and the book's editorial apparatus; the second between the poem and the commentary; and the third between the commentary and the index, which refers us back far less to the poem than it does to the notes. On first reading, of course, we hardly see the blank pages; we expect these clear demarcations in such a text. But by the time we finish *Pale Fire*, we discover that they mark not rational divisions but complete separations, the central separation governing the other two. If we now think about the text as a whole, we may describe these separations, empty spaces, holes, as presences in our reading experiences—to be encountered just as we usually encounter characters, action, description, dialogue, discourse, rhythm, or diction.

I am focusing on *Pale Fire* as a physical object not only to illuminate an important dimension of our reading experience but also to suggest a relationship between the choices of physical directions and the sets of psychological, epistemological, and ontological judgments that we will implicitly make—or between the direction in which we read the book and what the book means. For example, suppose, as a kind of thought experiment, we try to design an ideal reading of *Pale Fire*. How should we proceed? The first choice confronts us at the end of the foreword, when we turn into the empty pages that precede the poem. The editor has advised us to suspend our customary priorities and begin with the commentary. But what gives the editor the authority to advise us? He starts his foreword with the cool objectivity of an authoritative scholar (pedant), but soon his enthusiasm begins to intrude. We begin to wonder about the judgments of a man who has been compelled to leave an improbable New Wye and assume an incognito, who recalls a "glorious friendship" not mentioned in the poet's obituary (73), who treasures his first glimpse (from his second-story window) of "the poet's slippered foot" (15), who records the first words spoken to him by the poet—the laconic suggestion that he "try the pork" (13)—and the poet's spontaneous utterance when a snowflake fell upon his watch—"crystal to crystal" (14).

When, in our thought experiment, we pause in the empty space between the foreword and the poem, we discover that nothing we have read so far guarantees the right way to go on. The foreword has destroyed our sense of direction, or normal procedure; it has compelled us to make a decision and, at the same time, denied us any way of telling right from wrong. The decision we make at this conscious moment in our thought experiment, about which way to go through the novel, will imply at least a tentative judgment about Kinbote as a critical authority and, hence, about the judgments he makes within his commentary.

One of the judgments we may pause to consider, even before we get to the poem, is aesthetic. Is the poet's spontaneous utterance "crystal to crystal," when the snowflake lands upon his watch, poetry or posturing? And, we should ask as we read Shade's poem, is "Pale Fire" an elegant display of wit that fuses mundane reality with poetic fancy, as many readers contend? Or is it a preposterous display of egoism that puffs up stupid perceptions with poetic rhetoric, as may be suggested by such a mundane metaphor as "TV's huge paper clip" (24); by the fingernail clippings in which he discovers "flinching likenesses" of his grocer's son, the college astronomer, a tall priest, and an old flirt (28); by the details that would be overlooked by his "staid biographer"—the apparatus he designed for shaving in the bath, a

> Hinge-and-screw affair, a steel support
> Running across the tub to hold in place
> The shaving mirror right before his face
> And with his toe renewing tap-warmth, he'd
> Sit like a king there and like Marat bleed
>
> (46–47)

and by the discovery that his affinity with the woman who, like him had died and been reborn, was based on a misprint in the new-paper account of her vision:

> *Mountain*, not *fountain*. The majestic touch.
> Life Everlasting—based on a misprint!
> I mused as I drove homeward: take the hint.
>
> (44)

The aesthetic judgment—whether "Pale Fire" is a good or bad poem—determines how we read the book. It determines the ultimate narrator, controlling intelligence, arranger, who—though felt as a dramatic presence—is kept beyond our grasp, or within the empty spaces. The question of the ultimate narrator is opened in the lacuna of the poem's putative last line; indeed, we might see the hole between the poem and commentary opening not in the pages between them but in the space after line 999, which the heroic couplet form obliges to be filled in. Kinbote insists that line 999—"Trundling an empty barrow up the lane"—was to be followed by a repetition of line 1—"I was the shadow of a waxwing slain"—thus completing a perfect circle—and, we might add, completing the juncture between the mundane and the poetic. But there is another choice open to us by the lacuna. The commentary ends with Shade, who has become a shadow of Kinbote, being slain, if not "by the false azure in the windowpane" (line 2), then by the false reflection in the mind of the (imagined?) assassin. We may, therefore, see a bridge between the commentary and the poem, or a joining of the poem and the commentary into a perfect circle and, as a result, a unity of the poet and commentator.

But who is the primary narrator, guiding intelligence, arranger? The answer depends upon an aesthetic judgment. Readers who judge the poem to be an elegant work of art see Shade as the primary narrator, a poet capable of imagining the fantastic Kinbote and adding what his character Kinbote tells us is the human counterpart to the poem. Readers who assume the poem to be ridiculous see the primary narrator as Kinbote, a poet *manqué* or a paranoid, who has appropriated Shade's text and/or fantasized an ideal or two ideal selves.

But the aesthetic judgment is not so simple, and neither, therefore, is the locus of the primary narrator. The poem is neither elegant nor stupid. It is wildly comic but capable of constraining the most ornate diction and the most mundane perceptions, the most sophisticated allusions and the most slapstick descriptions, within its tightly controlled meter. The effect is most striking when the poem is read aloud.

Once we have developed a taste, like Aunt Maude's, "For realistic objects interlaced / With grotesque growths and images of doom" (25), once we laugh at the images and admire the interlacing, a signal question arises. Where in the world of *Pale Fire* do we find a character capable of such wit, such wild flights and mixtures, such control? Not in the dull gray poet characterized by Kinbote. Not in the persona of Kinbote as he exists in the commentary or in the foreword, who is so limited by his zeal and paranoia. And not in the persona of the poem, who takes his dull life so seriously and who enjoys his posturing as much as Kinbote admires it. We do not find the controlling intelligence in the foreword, the poem, the commentary, or the index.

Indeed, in the last paragraph of the commentary the narrator distinguishes himself from his fictional personae. He has just told us that his "work is finished": his "poet is dead," and he wonders (or postulates the inquiry of a "gentle young voice"), "What will *you* be doing with yourself, poor King, poor Kinbote?" Now he invokes God's help "to rid myself of any desire to follow the example of two other characters in this work. . . . I may assume other disguises, other forms, but I shall try to exist." Perhaps more important, he will remain inseparable from the counterpart, who "has already set out . . . and presently . . . will ring at my door—a bigger, more respectable, more competent Gradus" (212-13).

We may discover a clue to the controlling intelligence when the poet describes the major catastrophe of his life, his daughter's death or suicide. He refers to the improbable geography of his region:

> People have thought she tried to cross the lake
> At Lochan Neck where zesty skaters crossed
> From Exe to Wye on days of special frost.

(36)

Further, when called to lecture at the Institute of Preparation for the Hereafter, he notes his temporary move from "New Wye / To Yewshade" (36).

Here not the poet but the poem calls attention to itself as a product of language, indeed, of letters. Here the poem moves from the highest flights of poesy to the lowest ground of reality: the physical units that compose it. Here the book calls attention to itself as a physical object composed of discrete parts and empty spaces, composed primarily of a poem and a commentary and a hole between them. The hole in the center not only keeps the poem and commentary apart and the various doubles from ever merging. It also obscures the guiding intelligence who has engaged us by his comic powers, changing reflections, and diabolical control.

A "black hole" is the result of a gravitational field so intense that no light can escape. It is what astronomers call the absence they encounter in empty space. It is also an imaginative concept arrived at through the daring and skill of human intelligence able to destroy traditional forms and expectations and play with the possibility (indeed, necessity) of a star so massive as to collapse in on itself—before such a phenomenon could be searched for, let alone confirmed.

The black holes in *Lolita* and *Pale Fire* are similar, except that they implode not in outer space but in the realm of human experience. As a result, they threaten the bases of both rational explanation and humane judgment. In *Lolita* the narrator, laughing diabolically in the narrative black holes, leads us through an experience of longing and love while undermining our ability to measure it against traditional norms. In *Pale Fire* the narrator, laughing diabolically within the hole separating the poem from the commentary, denies us—indeed, forces us to continually question —all physical, psychological, epistemological, and aesthetic guidelines. The hidden narrators of *Lolita* and *Pale Fire* have cheated creation by creating a new life in each fiction—and by generating a new life in the readers, who, denied the security of habit, must see and decide for ourselves. The black holes in *Lolita* continually disrupt the narrative continuity and displace us from whatever vantage we establish. The black holes in *Pale Fire* continually compel us to choose a direction—that is, to become our own source of motive power. The novel in motion, having first engaged us along with the narrator in the act of excited perception and then confronted us with an unpicturable and unmanageable experience, now draws us in and makes us responsible for an experience that changes with each choice we make.

CHAPTER SEVEN

Where're They At, Where're They Going?
Thomas Pynchon and the American Novel in Motion

It may be a mark of overdeveloped sensibility, professional dysfunction, or sheer perversity; but it is common to hear from postmodernist critics that Thomas Pynchon is, after all, quite conventional—even in *Gravity's Rainbow*. In one sense this is true, and if I were not developing my argument more or less historically, I might put him before Joyce. For—despite the changes in point of view—Pynchon does not engage us in the movement of the narrative eye, nor does his narrator enter the frame of the story. In Pynchon's novel we focus on the story. We are engaged by the plot—by the sequence of events, what happens next, the movement of his characters—as well as the pervasive plotting of characters, organizations, and incalculable forces. Indeed, Pynchon develops, or overdevelops, his plots to the point where they become almost unbearable. That is, we feel the strain of their palpable movement. In this sense Pynchon is modern or postmodern, for he engages us in a dynamic dimension of his medium.

In this chapter I will distinguish between two kinds of plot development. The first, which I call *movement*, is traditionally logical, purposeful, and clear. The second, which I call *motion*, is alogical, unpurposeful, and confusing, for it develops through a series of unpredictable transformations. But the transformations are still sequential. Indeed, the power of Pynchon's novel in motion derives from their absolute succession, from one transformation completely succeeding another—from our being led forward from event to unpredicable event, place to unexpected place, the known to the unknown.

Walt Whitman, sounding his "barbaric yawp over the roofs of the world," invokes his persona, his subject, and the form of his poem as: "Nature without check with original energy." Thomas Pynchon, whose *Gravity's Rainbow* opens with "a screaming" that "comes across the sky," sounds a yawp that now makes Walt Whitman seem like the corresponding secretary of a 4-H club. He invokes the world of his novel with an epigraph by Werner von Braun: "Nature does not know extinction; all it knows is trans-formation."[1] In the century between "Song of Myself" and *Grav-ity's Rainbow*, a signal feature of American literature has been "Nature without check with original energy"—in works that strain at the seams, that defy critical description and judgment, that succeed out of their sheer bravado and power. The barbaric yawp issues from such brilliant failures as Hart Crane's *The Bridge* and William Carlos William's *Paterson*, from the monu-mental exuberance of Thomas Wolfe, from the kaleidoscope of Dos Passos's *U.S.A.*, from the page-long sentences of Faulkner's narrators as they try to grasp the ungraspable, from Henderson the Rain King's "grun tu molani," from the lyric obscenity of Norman Mailer's "disk jockey" evoking the myths and misdi-rected energy that brought us to Vietnam. The barbaric yawp gets louder and more dissonant. The unchecked energy becomes more potent and more destructive. And the writers deal with this energy in a much more ambivalent fashion. But our experience of this energy, or its very dynamic, also undergoes a change that is re-flected in the difference between Whitman's view of "Nature without check" and Pynchon's view of nature that only knows transformation. I will try to describe this change and develop an approach to *Gravity's Rainbow*, first, by distinguishing two forms that have given expression to America's unchecked energy—the novel of movement and the novel in motion—and, then, by describing Pynchon's encounters with unchecked energy in his three novels.

ENERGY, MOVEMENT, AND MOTION

Let me begin by trying to define my key terms. *Energy* is the power to move a work along; that is, to move language, character, action through the stanzas, chapters, or acts. It is also the power to produce effects, to move the audience to laughter, tears, pity, fear. All good literature, of course, is endowed with energy. But it is interesting that we become aware of the energy, or speak of the energy, when the power of a literary work begins to exceed its form. Doesn't the fastidious critic commend the energy just before deriding the style of, say, Dreiser's *American Tragedy* or O'Neill's

Long Day's Journey into Night? To return to Whitman for a moment, we begin to sense the energy of "Song of Myself" in the gaps between its discontinuous sections, stanzas, lines, or phrases, and in the discontinuities of its very grammar. On the opening page, for instance, we encounter a stanza that begins:

The smoke of my own breath,
Echoes, ripples, buzz'd whispers, love-root, silk-thread, crotch and vine,
My respiration and inspiration, the beating of my heart, the passing of
  blood and air through my lungs,

And that ends:

The feeling of health, the full-moon trill, the song of me rising from bed
  and meeting the sun.

Though there is a recognizable associative if not logical movement from one line to the next in most of the stanza, following from the image of breathing, and though most of the lines are contained by some unifying pattern, there is no recognizable link between the first two lines. And the elements of the second line—"echoes," "ripples," "buzz'd whispers," "love-root," "silk-thread," "crotch and vine"—seem unrelated. More important: the stanza is an incomplete sentence—a series of subjects with no predicate, noun phrases with no verb. We may even describe it as a series of substantives with the potency of verbs, where, as the substantives accumulate, the potency increases. It is in this sense that we recognize a work's energy as it exceeds its form, and it is in this sense that the poem is "Nature without check with original energy."

When we speak of *movement* in a literary work, we can be more precise, for movement is the continuous going from point to point. We can focus on *what is going* as well as on the *direction* and *pattern* of its *progress*. Although we can describe the movement in "Song of Myself" as the associative pattern of the poet's thoughts, the notion of movement, for reasons I shall come to, does not help us much with this poem. Therefore, let us turn to the novel, where we can more easily describe—or plot—the movement of characters through time and space. Let me illustrate this concept of movement and illuminate an important development in American literature that takes us in the direction of the novel in motion and *Gravity's Rainbow.*

F. Scott Fitzgerald's *The Great Gatsby* and Nathanael West's *The Day of the Locust* both deal with the energy that Whitman glorified and that, undirected or misdirected, has become destruc-

tive. Both writers show the destructive energy just barely suppressed and masked by the shimmering surfaces and tasteless
facades. Both writers connect this energy with their particular
visions of the American wasteland. Nevertheless, their visions
are different in ways that go beyond the details of locale or
history. We can describe this difference in terms of movement—or,
specifically, in terms of goals, vehicles, motive power, and ends.

The goal in *The Great Gatsby* is "the green light at the end of
Daisy's dock," which Fitzgerald compares to "the green breast of
the new world" that "flowered once for Dutch sailors' eyes."[2] The
goal of West's characters is Hollywood, with its "Mexican ranch
houses, Samoan huts, Mediterranean villas, Egyptian and Jap-
anese temples, Swiss chalets, Tudor cottages, and every possible
combination of these that lined the slopes of the canyon"—and, of
course, Faye Greener.[3] The vehicle for Fitzgerald is Gatsby, with
his "heightened sensitivity to the promises of life" (2), as seen
through the eyes of Nick Carraway, a sensitive outsider, rooted in
the topsoil of American society. West's novel contains a similar
observer in Tod Hackett, but it is important to note that there is no
sharply defined vehicle upon which he is focusing. The motive
power for Gatsby, and for Nick, is a Romantic striving; the motive
power for West's characters is a vague but powerful momentum,
sometimes described as the need to escape, sometimes as the drive
to succeed. The end of *The Great Gatsby* is the destruction of the
vehicle, the Romantic protagonist, and the recognition of lost
values—but the world remains intact. The end of *The Day of the
Locust* is apocalypse, the destruction of the characters and the
world of the novel.

Fitzgerald, whose vision of life conformed to the conventions of
historical evolution and the mechanics of cause-effect, makes the
dynamics of movement in the traditional novel graphically clear,
for he so clearly defines the goal, the vehicle, the motive power,
and the end. Fitzgerald's twenties may be symbolized in Gatsby's
yellow roadster speeding toward Daisy's home under the eyes of
T. J. Eckleburg. The vehicle *progresses* and *accelerates* along a
straight line until it goes *out of control* and *causes* destruction.

West's thirties may be symbolized in the riot that concludes *The
Day of the Locust*—the characters swirling irrationally with
increasing violence. West has experienced the loss of control and
the destruction evoked by Fitzgerald, and has at least sensed that
history does not progress and that effect does not so simply follow
from cause. As a result, he creates a pattern of movement that is

less easy to define. There is no vehicle. And though the novel is ostensibly linear (in that we follow the development of Tod Hackett from day to day), there is no direction, no meaningful pattern from point to point in the novel's space and time. To put it another way, the apocalyptic ending is not caused by any choice or event in the novel.

The Day of the Locust focuses on the motive energy rather than on a vehicle and its pattern of movement toward a goal; to describe the novel, therefore, we should speak not of movement but of motion. *Motion* is the process of movement without regard to what is moving. Its dynamic structure cannot be plotted in a purposeful or causal pattern; it can only be described as a field of forces or a process of transformations. When the transformations are irrational, when linking gives way to discontinuity and direction to aimlessness, we encounter the experience of "Nature without check with original energy."

"Song of Myself" is designed to give the illusion of motion rather than movement, and at some points, like the one I described, what we experience is actually motion. But if the movement of the poem lacks any apparent direction, the poem does have a coherence—indeed, it is about relationship; it does have a center—the mind of the poet; and it does have an associative if not logical pattern of motion. Whitman could glorify "Nature without check with original energy" because he was incapable of imagining nature without check, because he believed in an ultimate coherence. Fitzgerald could see and even plot the effects of nature without check or misdirected energy, but he could not focus on the energy itself. West could focus on the energy lyrically or symbolically but knew of no other way to handle it than within the framework of a traditionally linear novel. As Pynchon approaches *Gravity's Rainbow*, he realizes all the implications of "the original energy" that early writers could either not accept or not reflect in a literary form. He finally evolves a novel of motion rather than movement—a novel that abrogates direction, that focuses on the field of forces that governs contemporary life.

V.

" 'Where we going,' Profane said, 'The way we're heading,' said Pig. 'Move your ass.' "[4] Benny Profane, Pig Bodine, Happy Hod, Herbert Stencil, Sidney Stencil, Evan Godolphin, Hugh Godolphin, Paola Maijstral, Victoria Wren, Vera Meroving, Veronica

Manganese move their asses all over the place in Pynchon's first novel—continually going, or seeming to go, in no other direction than the way they're heading. Indeed, *V.* is about three kinds of movement that, when interconnected—or intercut—come together as unfocused, undirected, and ungovernable motion.

Benny Profane—a schlemiel but not a coward, capable of feeling but not of attachment, disturbed by the inanimate but not prepared to militate against it—rejects modern society by becoming a yo-yo. He rides the shuttle back and forth, accepting whatever comes his way—a job, a drink, a woman, a fight, a trip to Malta— but he is always ready to cut loose when the connection becomes too secure. In a threatening world, he maintains his equilibrium and a minimal identity by being constantly and aimlessly on the move. That the pattern of his movement is like a yo-yo suggests its psychological if not its geographical limits.

Opposed to Benny is Herbert Stencil, whose movement since 1945 has been constant but purposeful. "His random movements before the war had given way to a great single movement from inertness to—if not vitality, then at least activity. Work, the chase— for it was V. he hunted . . . for no other reason than that V. was there to track down" (44). The chase after V., with its ever changing direction and elusive goal, allows Herbert Stencil to maintain his equilibrium in a world of space and time that reaches far beyond Benny's, and to maintain a minimal identity—as a stencil.

The third kind of movement *V.* is manifest in the elder generation. Hugh Godolphin is an explorer. Sidney Stencil is a foreign agent, who goes wherever Whitehall tells him, and who "with no element to be out of" is "at home everywhere"—except, finally, in Malta (453). Victoria Wren, Vera Meroving, Veronica Manganese —or V.—ends up as an agent for Mussolini. Even more than Stencil, she has no element to be out of and is at home everywhere. Her movement comes to be defined as "tourism":

> V. at the age of thirty-three (Stencil's calculation) has found love at last in her peregrinations through (let us be honest) a world if not created then at least described to its fullest by Karl Baedeker of Leipzig. This is a curious country, populated only by a breed called "tourists." Its landscape is one of inanimate monuments and buildings; near-inanimate barmen, taxi-drivers, bellhops, guides. . . . More than this it is two-dimensional, as is the Street, as are the pages and maps of those little red handbooks. As long as the Cook's, Travellers' Clubs and banks are open, the Distribution of Time section followed scrupulously . . . the tourist may wander anywhere in this coordinate system without fear. . . . Tourism thus is supranational, like the

Catholic Church, and perhaps the most absolute communion we know on earth: for be its members American, German, Italian, whatever, the Tour Eiffel, Pyramids, and Campanile all evoke identical responses from them; their Bible is clearly written and does not admit of private interpretation; they share the same landscapes, suffer the same inconveniences; live by the same pellucid time-scale. They are the Street's own. (384)

"Tourism," as we find it implicitly amplified in *V.*, is a constant movement with constantly changing direction. But it differs from Profane's yo-yoism and from young Stencil's chase or search for V. in that it is not volitional, in that the motive energy does not come from within. Tourism is not a choice to escape or to pursue but to abdicate choice. It is an acknowledged or unacknowledged obedience—or the following of some authoritative and unquestionable set of directions. Such obedience may be judged harmless, if mindless, when the tourist follows a Baedeker. It may be judged benign if the agent as tourist follows the instructions of a "friendly" government. It becomes suspect when we begin to recognize the colonialist objectives of the "friendly" government, and it becomes fully malign when the agent's instructions come from Mussolini. The destructive potential—indeed, proclivity—of tourism is implied by the identification of Karl Baedeker with his fellow Leipziger, Kurt Mondaugen (212). For Mondaugen, who obediently travels to South West Africa in pursuit of atmospheric radio disturbances, is associated with the most explicit colonialism and the most frightening impulses of fascism.

Abdication of choice and of control leads to the loss of direction: we don't know where the characters are going, we can't tell the past from the present, we can't judge the political right from the political left, good from bad, comic from tragic. How are we indeed to judge the novel's climax: where Sidney Stencil (serving a government that would soon become an ally in the fight for freedom) and his former lover Veronica Manganese (serving an Italian faction not yet prepared to open a second front in the fight for total control) are both plotting to keep Malta free? And where they join forces to compel the double agent Fausto Maijstral to leave their respective services and rejoin his pregnant wife? And how are we to judge the novel's ending: where Fausto's daughter Paola decides to rejoin her husband, Pappy Hod? We can never understand the motivation of V., or of Paola, who gives V.'s ivory comb to Pappy Hod. That is, we can never understand what moves them or where they are moving.

By the end of *V.* there is a total confusion, or merging, of all moral directions, and we come to sense that the three different kinds of movement are one motion: the motion of unchecked energy. There is no difference among the choice of escape, the choice of pursuit, and the choice of giving up choices. To become a human yo-yo is as mindless as to pursue an elusive goal, or to become a tourist, or to become an agent. Each choice is as mechanical or aimless or menacing as that of SHROUD OR SHOCK, or Esther as she submits to a nose job, or V. as she displays her glass eye with the clock iris—or the children who leave their games to undress the wounded priest, dig the star sapphire from her bleeding navel with a rusty bayonet, and run off with the clock iris.

V. follows the capricious string of Benny's yo-yo and the trail of a woman whose name and shape are constantly transformed. We never know where we're going except that it's the way we're heading, and we're heading from place to place and time to time in ways that are often bewildering. Nonetheless, the novel is not without check, and in the end we know where we've been. For *V.* is governed by an omniscient narrator, who tells the story by intercutting one strand of the complex plot with another, but all along holds the story together in his mind and can tie up the loose ends in an epilogue. The first intercutting, of Rachel Owlglass and her MG into the story of Benny and Paola, is soon recognized to be a simple, associative flashback—"the sinister vision of Pig and that Harley Davidson alone in an alley at three in the morning" reminds Benny of Rachel and her MG (13). By the epilogue we discover that all the disturbing jumps in the multi-stranded narratives have been simple flashbacks—or intercutting or crosscutting from one plot line to another. The intercutting has been the narrator's way of reinforcing the enigma of V. and the confusion of moral direction. It has also been a technique designed to maintain suspense throughout the chase, or to keep the story moving.

It is important to recognize that the narrative crosscutting employed by Pynchon in *V.* creates the illusion of discontinuity while holding the novel in check or together. Indeed, it is like the crosscutting employed in the kind of chase scenes that influenced Pynchon: those that dominate or culminate the early movies. Crosscutting, as I have pointed out, is what effected the experience of the chase. Suspense is created as Griffith cuts back and forth between the helpless victim and her rescuer, but in the scene of the last-minute rescue, the two lines of action are drawn together. And while planning the crosscutting of four very different stories in *Intolerance*, each of which culminates in a last-minute rescue, he declared: the "stories will begin like four currents looked at from a hilltop. At first the four currents will flow apart, slowly and quietly. But as they flow, they grow nearer and nearer together, and faster and faster, until in the end . . . they mingle in one mighty river of expressed emotion."[5]

Narrative crosscutting, therefore, derives from a sense of purpose, a goal, and, in the novel, from the stable perspective of the narrator. At the end of Pynchon's first novel, V. remains an enigma: but what happens in the life of Herbert Stencil as he pursues her becomes clear, and the pattern of his movement secures the pattern of Benny Profane's. Moreover, the goal—where the crosscut plot lines are drawn together—and the sense of purpose implied in the narrator's design give coherence to the purposeless motion of the novel's characters and constrain the run-away energy. The main characters have been going in no other direction than the way they've been heading, but their paths culminate in a pattern that the reader can finally plot.

THE CRYING OF LOT 49

In Pynchon's second novel he abandons the stable omniscient perspective to focus on Oedipa Maas's developing consciousness; the narrator only knows what Oedipa knows at each step in her quest. The narrative proceeds not by the intercutting of plotlines but by the addition—indeed, overloading—of information into a simple linear plotline. Oedipa's quest, her movement and goal throughout the novel, is purposeful, as she tries to piece together and comprehend the limits of Pierce Inverarity's estate. But as the information accumulates, it undermines the purposeful movement of the plot line and evokes an experience closer to the dynamic of motion that Pynchon will achieve in *Gravity's Rainbow*.

The steps in Oedipa's quest can be laid out in a chronological sequence and geographically continuous pattern. One day she receives a letter naming her executor of Pierce Inverarity's estate. She drives from her home to the Echo Courts in San Narciso for a surprise meeting with Pierce's lawyer. Then she goes to the Scope, a bar near Yoyodyne (Pierce's aerospace empire), where she learns about the Tristero; to the Fangoso Lagoons, where she learns about Pierce's investment in bone charcoal; to a performance of *The Courier's Tragedy*, where she discovers the fictional or historical connections or parallels with the Tristero and the uses of bone charcoal; to Yoyodyne, where she learns about the

Tristero's current operations; through the city to discover a large but inconspicuous community that communicates through the Tristero's system of W.A.S.T.E. containers; to the home of Emory Bortz to learn about the Tristero's ancient struggle against the Thurn and Taxis; and finally to Ghengis Cohen's stamp auction to await the crying of lot 49—and what she hopes will be the ultimate piece in the wild jigsaw puzzle of Pierce's estate, Western civilization, and her own identity.

More important than the linearity of action is the linear development of Oedipa Maas from a flat caricature to a sympathetic and heroic character, and of her mechanical responses to a series of choices involving deep feeling and thought. She begins as a stereotype housewife returning from a Tupperware party where the hostess had put too much kirsch in the fondue, develops into a businesswoman bent on executing Pierce's estate, then into a woman driven by the need to know and finally by the need to connect. At the climax of her search, having discovered countless pieces of information, she comes upon a derelict sailor and is "overcome all at once by the need to touch him. . . . Exhausted, hardly knowing what she was doing, she came the last three steps and sat, took the man in her arms, actually held him, gazing out of her smudged eyes down the stairs, back into the morning."[6] The crying she awaits at the end of the novel, as critics have noted, reflects her compassion as well as her need to understand.

But the linear development of the plot—of the novel's action and of the protagonist—is only one dimension of *The Crying of Lot 49*; for as Oedipa discovers more information in her quest, she encounters kinds of plotting that are neither continuous nor progressive, and that defy the plotting of epistemological, ideological, or moral direction. After arriving in San Narciso and choosing a motel at random, she is surprised by the entrance of Pierce's lawyer, Metzger, who claims to have found her by scouring the motels all day. Her motel's TV is showing *Baby Igor*, an old film that Metzger claims to have starred in as a child. "Either he made up the whole thing, Oedipa thought suddenly, or he bribed the engineer over at the local station to run this, it's all part of a plot, an elaborate, seduction, *plot*" (18). And the commercials involve a plot with far wider scope than Metzger's seduction of Oedipa. Fangoso Lagoons and Beaconsfield Cigarettes are two of Pierce's interests. Beaconsfield Cigarettes use a filter made from bone charcoal. Much of the bone charcoal, we later learn, came through the Cosa Nostra from a lake in Italy, where a company of American troops had lost a battle to the Nazis in 1943. We also learn that a group of Wells Fargo riders had been massacred at one of the Fangoso lakes; the charcoal from their bones was used to blacken the faces of the killers in subsequent raids. Moreover, the bones of the ambushed battalion in *The Courier's Tragedy* had been fished up and turned into charcoal, which the Duke used for his perfidious correspondence.

At this point we might reflect on two kinds of plotting that are ingeniously confused in *The Crying of Lot 49*. First is the simple plotting of the novel's action and the protagonist's development—the rational plan, chronological sequence, progressive development of Oedipa's quest—to which is added the more rational but incredibly complicated plot of *The Courier's Tragedy*. Second is the plotting for salacious, commercial, and political ends—the rational planning and steps calculated to seduce Oedipa, sell products, secure markets, and establish empires. To these we might add a third kind of plotting, which is historical. As Oedipa picks up fragments of information that lead from her present to the past, she is driven by a stronger and stronger compulsion to connect the fragments into a rational order—to plot a causal sequence of events that would explain the present in terms of the past. But the more Oedipa learns, the more difficult it is for her, and for us, to make connections. The main reasons for this difficulty are the increasing amount of data and their increasing similarity. If we could only discriminate and define the opposing forces, we could discover what led to what. But the central problem for Oedipa, and for the reader who is limited to her perspective, is in defining—or plotting direction. We come to discover that historical or causal direction depends upon our ability to define values—or to plot ideological direction.

Throughout Western history, Oedipa learns, consolidation and system have given rise to individualistic rebellion, but we can never determine whether the rebellion is to the right or left. The Peter Pinguid Society, which is so conservative that it considers the John Birch Society left-wing, was founded by a man who opposed industrial capitalism—because it led to Marxism and was, therefore, part of the same "creeping horror" (33). Moreover, the struggle for freedom requires consolidation and system, but we can never tell whether the ultimate goal is liberty or tyranny. The novel focuses on what is central to both liberty and tyranny, the history of communication, or courier systems. The Tristero was a rebellious underground courier system that opposed the Thurn and Taxis (the established European mail service from 1300 to 1867); even when it appeared in America, it fought the established Pony Express and Wells Fargo disguised as blackfaced outlaws or Indians. But in the middle of the seventeenth century, during a period of Thurn and Taxis instability, the Tristero faced a major decision. The conservatives wanted to keep the Tristero radical, as the opposition to the established central mail service. The militant radicals wanted to join the Thurn and Taxis to make all of Europe dependent on them: "We, who have so long been disinherited, could be the heirs of Europe" (123). From this point on we cannot tell who is plotting against whom. Nor can we plot the ideological direction of the plotters. As a result, we can make no causal links—or fix the fragments of information into a graspable pattern.

When Oedipa encounters the community of silent dropouts, who communicate secretly and independently by subverting the interoffice delivery system of Yoyodyne, we are led to wonder if this is a comic triumph of the underground, or if W.A.S.T.E. is not finally the product of the giant aerospace corporation itself. One view leads us to a utopia of political, psychological, and sexual anarchism, and the other leads us to a frighteningly successful totalitarianism. When we remember that the unpredictable Pierce Inverarity held a large block of shares in Yoyodyne, we are led to see the whole affair as a hoax on the part of a man rich enough to buy a cast of thousands—and the threat becomes diabolic.

Pierce Inverarity is like V. in Pynchon's first novel, except that he is not the goal of the chase, nor do we ever see him, even. All we know of him is the disembodied voice that Oedipa recalls having awakened her at three in the morning a year before the action begins: "a voice beginning in heavy Slavic tones as second secretary at the Transylvanian Consulate, looking for an escaped bat; modulated to comic-Negro, then on into hostile Pachuco dialect, full of chingas and maricones; then a Gestapo officer asking her in shrieks did she have any relatives in Germany and finally his Lamont Cranston voice, the one he'd talked in all the way down to Mazatlán" (2-3). Lamont Cranston is radio's famous "Shadow," an invisible agent capable of appearing anywhere, anytime. Pierce Inverarity is introduced as a shadow undergoing continual transformation. Throughout the rest of the novel, he is identified only with San Narciso—the place to which Oedipa drives to begin her quest. San Narciso "had been Pierce's domicile, and headquarters: the place he'd begun his land speculating in ten years

ago, and so put down the plinth course of capital on which everything afterward had been built, however rickety or grotesque, toward the sky" (12-13). It was "less an identifiable city than a
grouping of concepts—census tracts, special purpose bond-issue
districts, shopping nuclei, all overlaid with access roads to its own
freeway" (12). As the novel develops, Oedipa learns that San Narciso has "no boundaries" in space or time (134).

Pierce Inverarity is shadowy and gratuitously protean; San
Narciso is abstract and limitless. Identified with Pierce Inverarity, San Narciso is not only the locus of the novel's action, it is
the bewildering field of its plotless plotting. It is also the shifting
ground of the novel's developing figure—the simple linear plotline
that identifies Oedipa Maas. As Oedipa pursues her quest—to
comprehend San Narciso—and gathers more information, an
agon develops between the novel's figure and ground. The figure
is continually threatened by the ground: the plot line is continually in danger of being absorbed by the plotless plotting. Oedipa
herself is in continual danger of giving in. If she could only give
in: "she had only to drift tonight, at random, and watch nothing
happen, to be convinced it was purely nervous, a little something
for her shrink to fix" (80). But if she did give in and drift at
random—like Mucho with his drugs, Hilarius with his paranoia,
Metzger with his opportunism, Jesús Arrabal with his political
persistence, or the dropouts who rebel against the system that
may be co-opting them—if she did give up her purposeful pursuit,
she would become part of the cast of aimless caricatures that form
the novel's ground.

Oedipa continues her pursuit: her mechanical response has developed into curiosity, and then into the humanistic need to know
and to connect; we follow the evolution of a self, or a self-
consciousness, that ultimately needs others to find the limits of its
identity. In the end Oedipa's purposeful movement remains distinguished from society's and history's senseless motion. The figure of the novel's plot stands out against the plotless plotting of its
ground. But the overall experience is not so simple or hopeful.

Stanley Koteks has introduced Oedipa to the concept of Maxwell's Demon, who by sorting molecules was suppoed to sustain
order and maintain the system's purposeful movement. The Demon, that is, was supposed to counteract entropy, the inevitable
development of disorder and exhaustion of energy. But Maxwell's
successors discovered that the new energy added to the system,
the mental energy required for sorting—gathering and piecing

together information—would only contribute to the mounting disorder, and thus to the entropy. And, as Anne Mangel points out in her instructive discussion of Maxwell's Demon in the novel, Oedipa in pursuing information and order only contributes to the disorder and entropy of her world.[7] By the end of the novel, Mucho has turned from her disk jockey husband into a solipsistic drug addict, Dr. Hilarius from her psychoanalyst into a madman, and Oedipa herself from a suburban housewife into an isolated fanatic driven by her vision of disconnection. In the end, that is, Oedipa stands out clearly against Pierce's formless San Narciso as does the path of her movement from the senseless motion that threatens to absorb it. But as the figure stands out against the ground, it is also disconnected from it. And the system as a whole is composed of disconnected fragments moving at different speeds in different directions—like the "anarchist miracle" of the deaf mutes dancing (97).

GRAVITY'S RAINBOW

"A screaming comes across the sky. It has happened before, but there is nothing to compare it to now."

"No light anywhere."

"He's afraid of the way the glass will fall—soon—it will be a spectacle: the fall of a crystal palace." (3)

The experience that generates *Gravity's Rainbow* is of not only the terror that pervaded England toward the end of World War II. It is of the acceleration of unprecedented events that have been occurring since then: the explosion of the atomic bomb, a "cold war" that created worldwide tension and paranoia, a Korean War that few people understood and the Vietnam War—which showed us how America's "original energy" had in fact been channeled into forms of exploitation and imperialism; which challenged America's image as the world's greatest power; which gave rise to riots in the ghettos, factionalism in our major institutions, and a revolution in taste and manners. This acceleration has also gathered impetus from computerization, space exploration, Watergate, the Arab oil takeover. On the one hand, we are living with the results of unchecked energy (and the metaphor has become frighteningly literal). On the other hand, we are living with the results of a galloping rationalism, which has sped up communication, made information as speedily available as it has opened up whole new areas of experience, and subjected us to an accelerated if undefinable control.

Gravity's Rainbow focuses on the V-2 rocket: "He won't hear the thing come in. It travels faster than the speed of sound. The first news you get of it is the blast. Then, if you're still around, you hear the sound of it coming in." "You couldn't adjust to the bastards. No way" (6, 21). Worse than the helplessness in an air raid is anticipating the new rocket—which travels with unprecedented speed, which abrogates direction through time and space, which denies logic, experience, and common sense. It explodes virtually before it arrives. How do you adjust to that? Indeed, it signals the fall of the crystal palace. And Pynchon evokes the spectacle in the very form and texture of his novel.

Let us begin where we should with a novel in motion, with general impressions; for it is these impressions that are memorable and that however difficult to grasp are the novel's subject matter. The story line of *Gravity's Rainbow*, unlike that of *V.* and *The Crying of Lot 49,* is unplottable. It lacks a central subject (vehicle), or even a hierarchy of subjects, and it moves from place to place without any apparent reason or purpose. First we center on Pirate Prentice, then shift to Roger Mexico, then to Tyrone Slothrop, whose love affairs take place in a pattern identical to that of the V-2 explosions. Now we think we have the novel's protagonist, and we watch him being pursued by the agents of Dr. Pointsman in the name of the war effort. But, as Slothrop's pursuers multiply and he escapes them (or thinks he does) in a white zoot suit, our frame of reference begins to shift. It shifts completely when he changes to a Wagnerian costume—a helmet with horns, a pair of buckskin trousers, a green cape emblazoned with a red R—to become Rocketman; and when he later disguises himself as a pig in a folk festival costume. Rocketman—pursued by agents of the right and of the left, and pursuing not only what will become the ultimate rocket of the future but the genesis of his own past—becomes the center of our attention for most of the novel. Then he disappears from sight, and our attention is centered now on the Russian Tchitcherine; now on the Nazi Captain Blicero (code name for Lieutenant Weissmann), who controls the ultimate rocket; now on the African Enzian, half-brother of Tchitcherine and former lover of Weissmann. And, as if this is not sufficiently confusing, we attend at one time or another to a cast of characters that takes up four double-columned pages in Scott Simon's useful index.[8]

Moreover, we are taken suddenly and erratically from London

to Holland, back to London, over to France, to Switzerland, and to "the Zone" of Occupied Germany—which, despite the enormous number and authenticity of details, loses its geographical locus and becomes as abstract as its designation. Now we are in the German sites, then back to London, and suddenly we end up in a California movie house. This does not take into account the innumerable dislocations, as we are shuttled into the past of hundreds of characters—or over to Africa, where black history seems to be developing to mirror the white history of Northern Europe. Nor does it take into account the dislocations in style—which shifts without signal, reason, or pattern, from involved to detached, from scientific to slang, from suspenseful narrative to popular song, from scrupulous realism to antic cartooning. What characterizes our large impressions of the plot, characterization, and style is dislocation, discontinuity, confusion; but it is also speed, directionless motion, and transformation. Let me develop this point by focusing on the novel's deceptively simple opening.

Gravity's Rainbow begins with a serious, realistic description of an evacuation. The "he," who has been afraid of the way the glass will fall, is absorbed into a "they," who travel by train through a dark countryside and stop at an unnamed city. They are taken up in a building filled with "thousands of . . . hushed rooms without light" (4). There is nothing to do but lie and wait, listening to the screaming of missles that have already exploded, wondering whether one of them will come in the darkness or bring its own light. Soon the "he" is again in focus and given a name, Captain Geoffrey ("Pirate") Prentice. We witness a scene where Teddy Bloat, hooked onto an ebony baluster by an empty champagne split in his hip pocket, begins to fall; and where Pirate "leaps off of the cot and kicks it rolling on its casters" so that "Bloat, plummeting, hits square amidships with a great strum of bedsprings" (5).

Before we follow Pirate to his rooftop banana garden, we may turn back to see how we got from "they" to "he" and from the hushed room, waiting in terror, to Pirate's antic maisonette. We must have missed something. But there's the link; it is italicized for us. The anonymous "they" are wondering and waiting for the light. And the next paragraph begins: "*But it is already light*" (4). As we sit looking at the italicized link, though, we discover that the transition is only syntactical—that the daylight came offstage, or offpage, that without our realizing it we have been transported in time and space. That indeed we have made what the physicist might call a quantum jump.

A quantum jump is the discontinuous movement of an electron from one ring of an atom to another, or the discontinuous transformation of an electron from one level of energy to another. The model of the quantum jump illuminates three important features of the opening pages, which Pynchon elaborates with even more imagination and daring in the course of his novel. First is the discontinuity: a quantum jump is a discontinuous motion or a discontinuous development. The novel, as we have seen, is discontinuous in terms of character focus, plot movement, and stylistic development. Second is the abrogation of direction: just as the rocket explodes before it seems to arrive, defying the directions of time and space, the novel moves from one place to another and from one time to another in all possible directions. Third, and perhaps most important, is transformation. Whether we describe the electron as circling on a new ring at a new speed or endowed with a new amount of energy, the electron—which is nothing but speed and energy—has been transformed. Our primary experience in the novel is of subjects and subject matter, which can be defined only in terms of speed and energy, undergoing constant and inexplicable transformation.

Gravity's Rainbow is about speed and energy, which Pynchon, like the modern physicist, sees as the basic reality. Like the modern physicist, Pynchon also forces us to discard those categories of thought that have mentally secured us, and accept a world where there are no links, no directions, but only continual transformation. Where Pynchon differs from the physicist is that he brings into his world the reality of politics and human values. He denies us the security of traditional forms, categories, directions, links—but forces us to sympathize, judge, and choose.

There seems to be no direction, no links, just random events. As Roger Mexico would have it, the world obeys only the law of probability. But, following the most disturbing transformation, lines come together, everything seems to be interconnected and to follow Pointsman's laws of cause and effect.

> Slothrop swings the long keychain of his zoot, in some agitation. A few things are immediately obvious. There is even more being zeroed in on him from out there than he'd thought, even in his most paranoid spells. Imipolex G shows up on a mysterious "insulation device" on a rocket being fired with the help of a transmitter on the roof of the headquarters of Dutch Shell, who is co-licensee for marketing the Imipolex—a rocket whose propulsion system bears an uncanny resemblance to one developed by British Shell at around the same time . . . and oh, oh boy, it just occurs to Slothrop now where all the rocket intelligence is being *gathered*—into the office of who but Mr. Duncan

Sandys, Churchill's own son-in-law, who works out of the Ministry of Supply located where but at Shell Mex *House, for Christ's sake. . . ."* (251)

But if so much is being zeroed in, who is zeroing in on whom? What is the ultimate source? Where does it all come together? Who's on what side? What's the ultimate goal? Where're they at, where're they going?

Escaping, perhaps, in Switzerland, Slothrop asks, "Why are all you folks helping me like this? For free and all?" "Who knows?" comes the answer. "We have to play the patterns. There must be a pattern you're in, right now" (257). *Gravity's Rainbow* draws us into a world of symmetrical, repetitive, but undefinable or unpicturable and unnavigable dynamic patterns. There is always a pattern that we are in, but the patterns are transformed, even when they seem to repeat themselves, and we never know how to evaluate the pattern we are in or how we have gotten from one to the other. The major pattern, of course, is the V-2 rocket, which, when it reaches its apex goes "pure ballistic"[7] and becomes that "purified shape latent in the sky" (209). The shape is like the distribution curve of the explosions, and throughout the novel we sense the threat of death and ultimate destruction, of inevitability, but also of random distribution or pure chance. On the other hand, the dominant pattern is also the shape of the rainbow, the shape of the Rocketman's helmet and horns, of Slothrop's erection; and we also sense throughout the novel the promise of sexual potency. The promise is sometimes perverted; most of the sexual force is associated with sadism, masochism, and destructive escalation. But the perverted sex is countered by the love of Roger Mexico and Jessica Swanlake, however ephemeral that may be.[9] It is also countered by the vitality of Tyrone Slothrop, not only in the joys and frustrations of his sexual encounters but in his pursuit of freedom and justice—just as the novel's darkness and despair are countered by its fecundity and comic spirit.

We have become accustomed to ambiguity in literature. Why, then, are we so disoriented by the ambiguity of *Gravity's Rainbow*? Perhaps because the novel is not ambiguous, or because we must reexamine the experience of ambiguity. *Ambiguous* derives from *ambi*, meaning "both," and *agere*, meaning "to drive." The root meaning forms an illuminating metaphor: to drive in both directions. Gatsby is ambiguous because his energy has been misdirected; in that sense we see him driving in both directions. Ambiguity, then, belongs to the novel of movement, where the choices, actions, and destinies of characters can be plotted, where the subject, or vehicle, is clearly delineated, and where it moves from point to point in a continuous direction. But in the novel in motion there is no fixed subject, continuity, or direction. The patterns are all there are: undefinable, unmeasurable, repetitive, symmetrical, overlapping, discontinuous, and unnavigable. And we have to learn to play the patterns.

The subject of *Gravity's Rainbow*, like that of *The Great Gatsby* and *The Day of the Locust* is the "original energy"—unchecked, directionless, and accelerating. Fitzgerald plots the effects of this energy in terms of classical movement. West evokes an experience of motion, but he contains the novel's energy in the form of the traditional novel of movement. With Pynchon we can say the energy exceeds the form, that is, if we consider form as a container. But Pynchon has finally developed a form the characteristic of which is not to contain. In *V.* he generated the experience of unchecked energy in the mindless movement of his characters. In *The Crying of Lot 49*, he thwarted the purposeful movement of his developing heroine by overloading information onto a simple plot line, or by undermining the plot line with a senselessly shifting ground. In *Gravity's Rainbow* he has composed a novel in terms of energy and motion and patterns undergoing constant, alogical transformation.

Slothrop learns that "the War has been reconfiguring time and space into its own image. The track runs in different networks now. What appears to be destruction is really the shaping of railroad spaces to other purposes, intentions he can only, riding through it for the first time, begin to feel the leading edges of. . . . " (257). In the past decade we have learned the same lesson. We may have also learned that our conventional ways of grasping history are inadequate and false because history cannot be grasped or contained as it moves forward from the known to the unknown. The experience of reading *Gravity's Rainbow* is like riding through modern history without the maps and seatbelts that have given us a false sense of security. And we can begin to feel the leading edges.

CHAPTER EIGHT

Robert Coover's Kaleidoscopic Spectacle

Pynchon's fiction embodies, not only America's unchecked energy and history's senseless acceleration, but the acceleration produced by a new communications technology. In the period following World War II, television, Xerox, new printing techniques, electronic circuitry, computers, and satellites were conveying such an overload of information that no single view could contain them. The mass media expanded and consolidated. The speed of communication, the quantity of information, and the power of the mass media extended the range of probability, destroyed the boundaries between fact and fiction, and leveled hierarchies of meaning and value. During the sixties we could watch the president of the United States being shot in a Dallas motorcade and then see it replayed in slow motion, stop motion, now from the high angle of a rooftop, now in extreme closeup—TV producers exploiting all the techniques that make baseball more interesting to watch in the living room than the stadium, and including the ads for Alka Seltzer and Ban deodorant. Before this vision faded from our minds, we could see Kennedy's assassin being killed "live" during a news conference. In a few years, after a spy story or a western, we would see a Vietnamese soldier being executed for the benefit of the NBC news cameras, and the picture would come to us through the same kind of satellite that would bring us the weather report. This was the decade that Americans shot civilians as well as soldiers in the name of pacification, and uprooted villages and devastated the countryside to preserve Vietnamese freedom. Young people grew all their hair out and wore flowery costumes to challenge America's puritanic values and the violence inherent in its dominant masculinity—only for long hair to become fashionable and for tie-dye tee-shirts to sell in expensive boutiques and the Sears catalogue. This was the period that culminated in an illegal plot organized by the Department of Justice as well as the CIA, employing a group of agents who bungled a break-in, one wearing an ill-fitting red wig, and where the president of the United States, who had always looked the part, emerged as the villain in what would have been a second-rate novel were it not so poorly conceived that it could never have sold.

History was becoming a spectacle, with many acts engaging our attention simultaneously. It was difficult to tell whether the acts were actual or fictional, produts of objective reporting or public relations, first- or third-rate showmanship, paranoid or truly mythic fantasies. It is just such a kaleidoscopic spectacle that Robert Coover invites us to attend in *The Public Burning*, as he looks back at the period that encompasses postwar American history.

The stage is set. Ethel and Julius Rosenberg, having been convicted on slim evidence of conspiring to steal atomic secrets and denied their final appeal by the Supreme Court, are about to be executed—on Times Square, which in its own way is "an American holy place long associated with festivals of rebirth."[1] An actual set is built at the intersection of Broadway and Seventh Avenue, an exact reproduction of the Death House at Sing Sing: "walls whitewashed and glaring lit, furnished simply with the old oaken electric chair, cables and heating pipes, a fire extinguisher, a mop and bucket for cleaning up the involuntary evacuations of the victims, and a trolley for carting the corpses off. The switch is visible through an open door, stage right, illuminated by a hanging spot" (4). The production is presided over by Cecil B. De Mille—with the assistance of Sol Hurok, Dan Topping, Bernard Baruch, the Atomic Energy Commission, Betty Crocker, Conrad Hilton, Sam Goldwyn, Walt Disney, Ed Sullivan, the director of the Mormon Tabernacle Choir, various chiefs of staff, the Sing Sing warden, the Holy Six, and many more. Every important figure in the free world will take part in the show. The area will be jammed for miles around. Mayor Impellitteri will sign a law permitting the sale of liquor in public theaters, and the whole of Times Square will be declared one; paper cups and ice will be dropped by helicopter, and whiskey will flow in through a kind of bucket brigade. An old panhandler will be set up with drinks faster than he can toss them down; he'll feel like the Bank of America, his pockets so heavy he can hardly move.

In the meantime, Uncle Sam is on the move—rescuing Czech refugee Jaroslav Lukas from his Russian kidnappers, rounding up the hundred escaped North Korean prisoners, shoring up the defense lines above the Hwachon Reservoir, infecting Albert Einstein with the flu, packing off the heaviest Berlin airlift of the year. "His eyes burning fiercely like Mandrake the Magician's, a transfiguring glory in his bosom and a wad of chaw in his jowls, he reaches up and out, seeming to stretch and grow, and with a smile of Christian charity lets fly the Pow'r that hath made and preserv'd us a Union: 'Whoopee-ti-yi-yo! its yore misfortune, little dogies, and none o' my own!' he booms from above, and—ka-BLAM!—decimates a whole paddyful of contentious gooks" (64).

And Richard Nixon, sleepless, unshaven (and looking like his own caricature), disheveled (with a broken fly-zipper), reads through the Rosenberg transcripts and FBI files for a clue, a plan, a chance to fulfill whatever destiny Uncle Sam has urged upon him at the Burning Tree golf course. He presses through traffic jams, against crowds, against good judgment, against all odds for a confrontation with Ethel Rosenberg just minutes before the execution is to take place.

Robert Coover's *The Public Burning* is as packed with authentic detail and authentic possibilities as *Gravity's Rainbow*. It too expresses America's original and uncontrollable energy. As Uncle Sam says to Nixon: "The earth belongs to the livin', boy, not to cold pickles! You can't tame what don't stand still and nothin' in this universe does! Einstein put his finger on it a long time ago—oh, he's gone off the deep end lately, I know, but listen, he knew what America was all about: don't let the grass grow under your feet! saddle up, keep movin', anything can happen!" (205). Like *Gravity's Rainbow*, it evokes the sensation of directionless and undirected motion through the very dynamic of its plot—through what happens next.

Anything can happen—which is an expression of America's boundless optimism and readiness for action. When Nixon steps off the train at Sing Sing, a false mustache pasted to his unshaven face and looking as improbable as Gorden Liddy would look with his red Watergate wig, he feels like "one of those beardy desperadoes arriving at a dusty Hollywood cowtown for the final showdown" (359). Suppressing his exhaustion, doubts, and self-consciousness, he is quickened by the experience of crisis: "There were no scripts, no necessary patterns, no final scenes, there was just *action*, and then *more action*! Maybe in Russia History had a plot because one was being laid on, but not here—*that was what freedom was all about*! It was what Uncle Sam had been trying to tell me: *Act—act in the living present!* I'd been sitting around waiting for the sudden inspiration, the stroke of luck, the chance encounter, forgetting everything that life had taught me. . . . I had to get up off my ass and *move*" (362). But *The Public Burning* is not only about movement, it is all motion. The plot drives toward a climax that neither Nixon nor the reader can anticipate. It encompasses what seems like all that happened in 1953 and foreshadows what will happen at the end of Nixon's career, but it moves through them at a breathless pace, quickened by slapstick scenes, montage, and intercutting, and climaxes in a devastating apotheosis.

The major dynamic of intercutting is achieved by the alteration of narrators. In one chapter we glimpse the broad perspective: the narrator, omniscient and detached, but speaking in the present tense like a hyped-up commentator in the *March of Time*, leaps from place to place and tells us what is happening on every front. In another chapter we hear Richard Nixon speaking in the past tense in the voice that narrated *Six Crises*; having learned confidence, coolness, and courage, he tells us what happened with an ambiguous sincerity that reflects his shallowness and opportunism, his innocence and awkwardness, his self-consciousness and isolation. Indeed, it is Coover's achievement to create a Richard Nixon who is at once blind and sensitive, a man of courage and a schlemiel, a caricature and a believable character, contemptible and yet sympathetic. Our equilibrium is continually upset by shifting from the present to the past, from the broad to the narrow, from one facet of Nixon's perspective to another.

The plot line, then—which shows Nixon driven by ambition and a sense of manifest destiny and racing against time toward some unknown goal—is impelled by the intercutting, as in D. W. Griffith's last-minute rescues. But the action is halted three times for a variety of intermezzos: "The War between the Sons of Light and the Sons of Darkness," where Eisenhower's speech taken verbatim from his public papers is reprinted in poetic stanzas to focus the inanities; "The Clemency Appeals: A Dramatic Dialogue by Ethel Rosenberg and Dwight Eisenhower," where the President never addresses the Prisoner or even acknowledges her presence as she tries to reach him; and "Human Dignity Is Not for Sale: A Last-Act Sing-Sing Opera by Julius and Ethel Rosenberg." The intermezzos, especially as they stand out typographically in the text, may remind us of the kind of set pieces Bertolt Brecht intruded into his dramas for their alienation effect. They do draw us out of the drama, which, given its fantastic nature and contemptible hero, we are surprised to discover has drawn us in. But they do not, like Brecht's intrusions, cause us to step back and take stock of the social reality that the drama parodies. Quite the contrary, they compel us to recognize the spectacle as including historical reality, the factitious reality of mass media and pop culture, a mythic nightmare, and a comic text—all inseparable.

The Public Burning is a kaleidoscopic spectacle with many acts, some occurring simultaneously, some succeeding one another with senseless momentum, seen now from afar, now from close up, a spectacle that draws us in as it draws us away, and that includes actual facts, parodied facts, fantasized projections, and its own artifice as part of the total reality. In reading it we are like the man emerging from the Trans-Lux three-dimensional production, "still somewhat possessed by the images of famous historical persons going up in flames, their waxy faces melting horrifically, their stiffened bodies crashing forward into his lap"—and having forgotten to remove his 3-D glasses. "He has had no difficulty in bringing the two film images together in the theater, and in fact he still has an ache in his forehead and the back of his neck from trying not to flinch when the fellow with the bat and ball started whacking the thing right between his eyes, but now, tumbling along out here on the street, he seems to see two separate and unassimilable pictures, each curiously colored. Everything is flat, distances are deceptive, and he keeps crashing into people, getting angry wary stares in reply" (283–84). But by the time he gets to Times Square, "he is no longer surprised by these ocular reversals, in fact he is very clear-headed, which is the main cause of his panic. It strikes him that he is perhaps the only sane man left on the face of the earth" (287).

The Public Burning is like Robert Altman's wide-screen spectacles *Nashville* and *Buffalo Bill and the Indians*. Like Coover, Altman focuses on spectacles that have mythic reverberations in America, and that are displays of ultimate showmanship. *Nashville* focuses on the "Grand Old Opry." It is about the showmanship of country-western performers that masks the emptiness of their lives, and sometimes their music (the unevenness of the music is not a flaw in the film). It is also about the power they exercise over Middle America, and the inclusion of a presidential campaign within the country-western spectacle adds a frightening dimension. *Buffalo Bill and the Indians* is about the showmanship of a figure who was never more than a character in a

Wild West show, who in fact was the invention of a pulp writer and a public relations man, and who as a prototype for the western hero exercised such power over the American imagination. It is also about the American Indian, who has been known only in terms of his performance in the westerns that Buffalo Bill's show inspired.

But Altman does not only focus on spectacle, he conveys the sensation of spectacle directly. He fills the wide screen and keeps a variety of events in focus. There is no center, everything is happening at once. We are engaged by any number of events simultaneously and try to follow the dialogue amid a welter of movement and noise. Nor is there any depth. Everything is there, the background as important as the foreground. And we can never get beyond the performers—well-known performers acting as themselves or as other characters but unable to escape the roles by which they are known; Paul Newman playing Buffalo Bill with depthless blue eyes surprises us with his acting ability but never ceases to be Paul Newman. Most important, the very depthlessness and dimension of the wide screen is always a part of our consciousness. As a result, we experience the sensation of motion—not through the movement of the camera eye, shifting perspectives, montage collisions, radical discontinuities, or senseless transformations—but through attending to the kaleidoscopic spectacle on the surface of the wide screen. Our equilibrium is continually upset as we shift our attention—and with it our critical judgment.

The novel cannot attain anything like the simultaneity of film; one event must succeed another. Nonetheless, Coover does effect something like Altman's cinematic spectacle by stretching the screen of our imagination, filling it with characters and events, and then cutting back and forth among them fast enough to keep them all fresh if not present while denying us any center of focus.

His first novel, *The Origin of the Brunists*,[2] engages and disturbs us for just this reason. Chapter one opens with a wide view of West Condon; the narrative eye moves quickly from point to point, sketching in the general outlines of the mining town and then filling it with characters. In the first ten pages we are introduced to the newspaper editor, his assistant, the coffeeshop waitress, Osford Clemens, Pooch Minicucci, Angelo Moroni, Vince Bonali, Giovanni Bruno, Preacher Collins, Toni Rosselli, Mike Strelchuk, Joe Castiglioni, Ben Wosznik, and Eddie Wilson. Some of these characters speak only a few lines or engage in only a bit of action, but others are physically described and even given a past. We know from the prologue, which dramatized "The Sacrifice," that Giovanni Bruno will become the Brunist Prophet, but he plays a minor role in the first chapter, occupies only a small space on the wide screen of our imagination, as it fills up—like Altman's—in a manner that prevents us from distinguishing major from minor. Then, after we are taken into the mine and begin to form a coherent picture, there is a sudden shift. Chapter two opens with a rapid series of close-up fragments, focusing now here, now there, now on a character we know, now on someone new, now picking up what may be description or unattributed dialogue, and printed in a way that brings the text itself into our consciousness:

> There was light and
> post drill leaped smashed the
> turned over whole goddamn car kicking
> felt it in his ears, grabbed his bucket, and turned from the face, but then the second
> "Hank! Hank Harlowe! I cain't see nothin'! Hank?"
> Vince Bonali knew what it was and knew they had to get out. He told Duncan to keep the boys from jumping the gun and went for the phone in
> saw it coming and crouched but it
> "Wet a rag there! Git it on your face!"
> seemed like it bounced right off the
> Red Baxter's crew had hardly begun loading the first car when the power went off. Supposed the ventilator fan had stopped working, because the phone
> "Jesus! Jesus! Help me! Oh dear God!"
> came to still holding the shovel but his
> looked like a locomotive coming (40)

Then the pace of the cutting slows, but not too much, as we are taken from one section of the mine to another, from one miner's consciousness to another, now coming up to hear the reports coming in, now catching a glimpse of what turns out to be a basketball game in the high school gym, now focusing on two of the miner's children necking in an old car. Strelchuk sees "Joe Castiglione with a piece of timber stove clean through him and Tuck Filbert smack up aginst the roof, his head upsidedown." He finds Preacher Collins with his leg pinned under a dislodged timber. "He didn't know what he was going to do. Collins' whole leg must have been no more than a quarter-inch thick from the knee down. Terror gripped Strelchuk and made him shake." Then a short break in the text and: "Thrust up by a whistle burst, lifted by the taut jack of forced silence, the ball leans over its zenith, sinks briefly, then springs from a finger's jar toward the Tucker City basket, into the hands of a black-jerseyed West Condoner. A roar. A bounce. A pass. Gyrating patterns as fingers trace spiraling fences around the black-trunked bodies. Drive. Retreat. Pass. Jump. Shot." Then another break, and: "Parked in an unlit corner of the lot outside the West Condon High School auditorium, the two receive the Word: *She is spreadin' her wings for a journey.* . . . Their bodies formed a convoluted 'X,' the figure of a Greek *psi*, he seated, boy's unchastised legs pushed forward under the dash, she curled across his lap and facing him." And then down into the mine again, where Eddie Wilson prays "into the radiant cloud for deliverance from despair" (43–44).

The Origin of the Brunists focuses on a spectacle of a religious cult forming in a small mining town, with all the histrionic elements magnified in the mass media, and it effects the sensation of spectacle in our reading experience. Even before the spectacle of the mine disaster, in the novel's prologue, we are presented with the spectacle of a sacrifice that will occur later: the Brunists, clad in their white tunics, are returning from the Mount of Redemption, where they have made preparations for tomorrow's event— the end of the world. They encounter a line of cars, the militant Common Sense Committee. Suddenly, amid the blazing headlights and crashing fenders, Marcella Bruno is seen lying in the ditch, her face serene but her small body grotesquely twisted in its white tunic. The novel reaches its climax the next day on the Mount of Redemption, as the Brunists await the end of the world, Marcella's dead body in a fresh white tunic, too big for her, laid out on a lawn chair, a silver candelabra at her head, crowds milling around eating peanuts and cotton candy, reporters popping flashbulbs, helicopters circling overhead, a TV outfit at work, the whole event being described over a loudspeaker.

Between the spectacle of the sacrifice and the spectacular carnival, which culminates in an apocalyptic melee that would have been beyond Nathanael West's wildest dreams, we are taken back in time. We are shown the mine disaster and the forming of the cult as well as its opposing faction, and we are engaged in the story from the viewpoints of innumerable characters from every class of society and every persuasion. Indeed, the picture we form of West Condon and the origin of the Brunists continues to widen—to the point where every character is both a significant participant and a minor, even comic, actor. As a result, Coover goes beyond Altman to expand our sympathies while at the same time sharpening our judgments and leaving us with a sense of sheer breadth.

The Universal Baseball Association, Inc., J. Henry Waugh, Prop.[3] is also filled with an enormous cast of characters. We come to know Henry, his friend Lou, his occasional lover Hettie, his boss Zifferblatt, and more than seventy players in his league plus the commissioners and managers. Once again Coover focuses on a spectacle of showmanship with mythic reverberations in America. "There were things about the games I liked," Henry tells us. "The crowds, for example. I felt like I was part of something there, you know, like in church, except it was more *real* than any church, and I joined in the score-keeping, the hollering, the eating of hot dogs and drinking of Cokes and beer, and for a while I even had the funny idea that ball stadiums and not European churches were the real American holy places" (166). His second novel, though, may seem more sharply focused than the first because it is narrated until the final chapter from the viewpoint of the proprietor of the Universal Baseball Association. But the spectacle includes more than the league that Henry creates and the games that he imagines with the aid of his records, dice, and charts. That is, it includes more than the breadth of Henry's vision and the events of his life. It includes the forming of the Universal Baseball Association. And this forming includes the creation of a history, governed by choice as well as chance, a history where the past continually grounds the present, where the present includes what happens in Henry's mind as well as what happens in his actual life as an accountant, where the present is continually turning into a future, and where the ultimate present includes our reading of the novel. Our sense of spectacle, then, is both wide and long— spatial and temporal. It comes, not from witnessing innumerable events from various perspectives as in *The Origin of the Brunists* and *The Public Burning*, but from our being engaged in the perspective of the character who creates the spectacle like a god, witnesses it like a spectator, participates in it like a vulnerable player, and finally leaves us without his presence but with his consciousness as it brings the past into the ongoing present.

Henry Waugh is an accountant, keeping the records of an anonymous firm in a nondescript office, but every night he goes home with his delicatessen sandwiches and beer to his Universal Baseball Association. The game he has created is regulated by three dice that advance the players in fifty-six possible ways, a Stress Chart to trigger more spectacular events when he rolls triple ones or sixes, and a Chart of Extraordinary Occurences when he rolls the triple twice in a row. But the choices are also governed by the players' records, which help him decide who will be on the starting line-up, who will substitute for whom, who will go in to pitch. The dice and charts, then, provide only the mechanics. The records provide the limits and possibilities, and the names provide the real drama. "You roll, Player A gets a hit or he doesn't, gets his man out or he doesn't. Sounds simple. But call Player A 'Sycamore Flynn' or 'Melbourne Trench' and something starts to happen. He shrinks or grows, stretches out or puts on muscle" (47).

Henry has been playing the game and keeping the records for fifty-six seasons, and during the past two months he has been playing so intensely that he has been speeding up time; the seasons are getting shorter and shorter. As the novel opens, Damon Rutherford, son of the all-time great Brock Rutherford, is pitching a no-hitter, a perfect game. To celebrate, Henry goes to Jake's bar; it is really Pete's but he calls him Jake—a long-standing but one-sided joke, Pete looking like the second baseman in Henry's league, who years back began running a bar near his team's ball park. After a good many drinks, he brings home an old friend, a hearty but aging B-girl. As he brings her into his apartment, he brings her into the world of the ballpark: "Hettie Irden stood at the plate, first woman ballplayer in league history, tightening and relaxing her grip on the bat . . . "(27).

The comic montage of action and wordplay may be seen as issuing from Henry's drunken confusion, just as the whole novel could be seen as Henry's losing control of reality and becoming lost in the world of his fantasies. But such a reading fails to account for the novel's widening dimension. In the scene with Hettie, the spectacle, and our perspective, is widening to include the reality of Henry's life and the reality of his fantasies. Indeed, the novel as a whole embodies two spectacles—or two acts within a larger, ongoing spectacle—and as spectators we continually turn from one to the other and occasionally grasp the spectacle as a whole. One act is a mythic American tragedy, like that dramatized by such writers as Melville in "Bartleby the Scrivener," Dreiser in *An American Tragedy*, and Arthur Miller in *Death of a Salesman*. It is the tragedy of the little man overcome by the reality of urban America and the fantasies generated by the American dream. The other act is the spectacle of baseball, which has become part of the American mythic consciousness, and which masks American reality in the guise of an American dream. The spectacle as a whole is governed by the League's proprietor, who is at once its creator and its victim.

Henry, an accountant by trade and inclination, has a passion for order, which draws him to baseball. "American baseball, by luck, trial, and error, and since the famous playing rules council of 1889, had struck on an almost perfect balance between offense and defense, and it was that balance, in fact, that and the accountability—the beauty of the records system which found a place to keep forever each least action—that had led Henry to baseball as his final great project" (19). But things fall apart. The center cannot hold when Damon Rutherford, now at bat—young, handsome, popular, self-assured, with two world's records riding on the game—is killed by the accident or malevolence of Jock Casey's "bean ball." Henry had seen the possibility on the Chart of Extraordinary Occurences. One chance out of 216. But the possibility becomes a reality, and the reality comes to include both the world of the ballpark and the world of Henry's daily life. Everything in the League goes awry. Chancellor McCaffree feels that it is "out of our hands, some built-in flaw or gap which doesn't allow us to cope with it. . . . It would almost be better for the whole league if the players were all incompetent or irrational" (149). If Henry himself had not known better, "he'd suspect the dice of malevolence rather than mere mindlessness" (152). When Hettie discovers that what keeps Henry busy every night is just a game, she opens her baggy jaws and whoops; her laughter tears clean through him (174). Good-natured Lou, trying to assuage what he thinks is Henry's loss of a friend or relative, joins in the game, but he lacks the patience and cannot take it seriously. He chooses players without regard for their histories and without thought to the future innings. He disrupts the game by describing a movie about a bee-girl (a transformed queen bee) while asking Henry from time to time about his B-girl. Then he spills his beer over all the records. And now, with Lou gone and the game in a shambles, Henry contributes to the disorder by imposing himself, and his own order, into the game. He changes the dice, giving York and Wilson back-to-back homers, setting the odds against the team responsible for Damon Rutherford's death, and moving the game over to the Extraordinary Occurence Chart. It is "as easy as that." But it is not that easy to go all the way, for now Jock Casey is on the mound, and Henry has the chance to even the score with the player who killed Damon Rutherford. "If you killed

that boy out there, then you *couldn't* quit . . . you'd be hung up
for good" (201). Henry tries to sleep, but he sees them waiting for
him out on the field. He sets out three sixes, Royce Ingram kills
Jock Casey with a line drive, and the epic era of the Universal
Baseball Association comes to an end.

Barney Bancroft will write the new league history. "It was all
there . . . in the records, but now it needed a new ordering,
perspective, personal vision, the disclosure of pattern, because
he'd discovered—who had discovered? Barney maybe—yes
Barney Bancroft had discovered that perfection wasn't a thing, a
closed moment, a static fact, but *process*, yes, and the process was
transformation" (211–12). Henry gives way to Barney Bancroft,
and he will soon disappear from the novel. Henry's account of the
Universal Baseball Association gives way—is transformed into—
Bancroft's "compact league history," which, as we immediately
leap into the next century, becomes an ancient and sacred text,
already giving way to interpretation and cynicism. But we must
remember that Barney Bancroft is Henry's creation, as is the
transformed league that continues in time. And if the time
through which it continues is not real, it is as Henry says
"*significant* time" (217).

Its significance is underscored by the fact that the last chapter—no longer focusing on Henry but possibly on the product of
his consciousness—is narrated in the present tense. It is now a
hundred years since Damon and Casey were killed, and we are
witnessing the ritual reenactment of the two games that ushered
in the new era. We are also engaged in a moment in history—the
novel's only pure present—that joins the old with the new, the
past with the future, what happened with what might happen.
That is, we are engaged in the very historicity of the present. The
old world has been transformed by the players, who are divided
into Damonites and Caseyites, two cults that have long since
drifted from their original values, and have even given rise to the
belief that Damon and Casey may never have existed, that they
were only myths. The new players are rookies, descendents of the
original players, who take on the original roles. But according to
the rules, no one can play his progenitor, so Melbourne Trench's
great-great-great grandson is playing Hardy Ingram's great-
great-great grandfather, the man who killed Jock Casey. And
Hardy Ingram is playing Damon Rutherford. Damon Rutherford
had no descendents but his spirit fills the ball park. No one knows
who is playing mad Jock Casey. So the spectacle is confused: the

transformation from past to future is being kept alive in the present. We must keep track—create our own ordering—or try to keep track of who is playing whom. No one knows what is going to happen—whether Casey will bean Damon again, whether Ingram will kill Casey again, whether the ritual will be real or just a game. It is important that we are confused, for as the novel moves from the past to the present tense, from Henry's account to an unmediated narrative, we participate in the confusion we had attributed to Henry. And it is important that in the end the game is just beginning, for the process is still in process, history is still being made, the spectacle is still alternating between the game and life and includes the very text of the novel. Paul Trench—playing Hardy Ingram, having originated in the mind of Henry Waugh and existing only in the novel whose pages we feel to be diminishing—wants to quit. He wonders why he keeps going: "The game? Life? Could you separate them?" (238).

In *The Origin of the Brunists* Coover fills the screen of our imagination and widens it by presenting a historical spectacle from the viewpoints of so many characters that we lose our center of focus and cannot tell the significant participants from the minor, even comic, actors. In *The Universal Baseball Association*, he widens the screen of our imagination by picturing the spectacles of an American Tragedy, a mythic baseball league, and a myth of creation. He also lengthens what we envision in time by engaging us in the league's history, in the very *process* that joins—at every point in the spectacle—the past to the present as it thrusts into the future. As Coover emphasizes in the novel's epigraph from Kant's *Critique of Judgment*, "It is here not at all requisite to prove that such an *intellectus archetypus* is possible, but only that we are *led* to the Idea of it" (my emphasis). As we are led to it, the possibility enters into the reality of a continuing present, which includes what happened or may have happened, what is happening or could be happening, and what may come.

Again Coover forces so much into the screen of our imagination that we lose our center of focus; in this case it is not only the enormous cast of characters and events but the breadth of a triple spectacle and the length of its duration. We also begin to lose our sense of boundaries—of where the screen actually ends. We cannot tell the game from life, the reality of the complex American myth. Nor, given the shift in the final chapter from the narrative past to the narrative present, do we have a temporal center—can we tell the reality of the past from the reality of the present or the reality of the future. And to this range of possible realities we must add the reality of the novel itself. Although the final chapter may be the product of Henry's consciousness—after all, every character and the ultimate event derived from what Henry created—we are left with the presence of the narrator who has silently mediated what Henry saw and thought. Henry is absent from the text, and, as we attend to the voice of the storyteller, we sense the possibility—the reality—of Henry's being his creation.

After *The Universal Baseball Association* and before *The Public Burning*, Coover experimented with a series of stories in *Pricksongs and Descants* that explicitly compel us to attend to the reality of the story as story.[4] One of the most remarkable stories is "The Babysitter," which not only denies us a center, destroys spatial and temporal boundaries, and confuses realities, but brings real and imagined events occurring in different places into the ongoing reality of the printed text. If this domestic spectacle is limited in scope and duration, it does include the mass media myths of popular culture. And if it is played out on what is more like a television screen than the wide screen of a movie theater the channels shift continually and arbitrarily to increase its range and add to the kaleidoscopic movements.

At 7:40 the babysitter arrives at the Tuckers and waits for them to finish dressing. Harry thinks, or perhaps sings, "That's My Desire," smiles toothily, pulls on his shorts, rubs his balding head, and gives his hips a slap. Jack thinks about his girlfriend babysitting at the Tuckers and drifts toward the drugstore. The babysitter catches a glimpse of Mr. Tucker hurrying out of the bathroom in his underwear. Bitsy and Jimmy, scheming at the kitchen table, picture "Her tummy. Under her arms. And her feet. Those are the best places" (207). Harry "catches a glimpse of the gentle shadows amid her thighs, as she curls her legs up under her." Or perhaps it's not Harry but the babysitter imagining how she'd entice him. "He stares hard at her. He has packed a lot of meaning into that stare, but she's not even looking. She's popping her gum and watching television. She's sitting right there, inches away, soft, fragrant, and ready: but what's his next move. He [but suddenly we discover that we have been in Jack's mind, all the way across town] notices his buddy Mark in the drugstore, playing the pinball machine, and joins him. 'Hey, this mama's cold, Jack baby! She needs your touch!' " (208). Now Mark joins in the chase that bounds from one character's viewpoint to another's and from one level of reality to another—from what seems to happen to what may be a character's fantasy-wish or fantasy-fear that he or she is chasing or being chased, catching or being caught, sometimes with hilarious consequences, sometimes with nightmare violence, sometimes the same event being replayed within the frame of another character's vantage and in a different key, sometimes an element of one character's fantasy or reality entering into another's as when Mark lifts the babysitter's skirt to see the big pair of men's shorts that she had tried on before taking a bath or imagined she did, continually being intercut with chase scenes from the western, murder mystery, and love story that alternate on the television screen in the living room, and continually alerting us to the playfulness of their creator, the narrator who develops the story as if he were switching TV channels at random.

Actually, "The Babysitter" has a simple, linear plot line that includes two subplot lines. The major plot line follows the babysitter from the time she arrives at the Tuckers' until they return. The minor plot lines follow Harry and Dolly to the party and Jack and Mark as they play pinball, call the babysitter, and perhaps go to see her. The linearity is underscored by continual time references: 7:40, 8:00, 8:30, 9:00, and finally, to our surprise after so much has happened, 10:00. But imposed upon the linear plotline is a series of alternating frames, each of which encloses us within the real or imagined perspective of a different character, and sometimes of the narrator himself, who is capable of intercutting—within a sequence of wild chases, comic seductions, and violent rapes in the Tucker living room and bathtub—a scene at the party where Dolly, having loosened her girdle for a few deep breaths and unable to pull it back up, is helped back into it by the other guests who must first lubricate her with melted butter. As a result of the shifting frames, the story is impelled through space and time in innumerable directions; and though we are impelled along the linear plot line, we are also impelled, when the perspective shifts midparagraph, to read back, or think back, and fill in the frame with different characters.

I use the term *frames* not just figuratively to suggest the shifting frames of reference that fracture the story's plot line but to describe the printed text, which becomes part of the reading experience. It is composed of short, discrete, frame-like blocks (from two to fifteen lines each), separated by three heavy dots. Each block literally frames an event or part of an event in its present tense. We are impelled to read across the dots as if they were ellipses, standing for what is left out and ensuring continuity through time and space. But we discover that the dots are not signs of continuity, that the pronoun now stands for a different person, that we are no longer in the same place, that we have been impelled into another present moment. We can never get beyond the present, beyond the frame—which includes what seems to happen, what seems to be imagined, and what may be created arbitrarily by the narrator. Each of these *events* is equally *there*, and hence, equally real. And the reality includes the event of the telling of the story and the event of its being shaped into a series of printed, framing blocks of text. Everything is brought onto the same level—indeed, onto the surface. We are impelled back and forth across the surface of the text. We can never get beneath it to discern what we have been accustomed to consider levels of meaning, nor can we get beyond the frame or surface to locate the narrator or his intention.

Coover does not continue in the same direction in *The Public Burning*, his most ambitious work to date and a major novel of the 1970s, where he returned to a wide-screen vision of American history. But his experimentation did add to the range of narrative techniques that impel the kaleidoscopic spectacle. He does intercut reality, fantasy, and myth to expand the range and increase the momentum of Nixon's senseless chase, and he does engage us in the reality of the text in his intermezzos. Moreover, his experiment with the dynamic potential of his medium may have contributed to a deepened awareness of America's misdirected energy and complex superficiality and, hence, to his vision of American reality of a pop nightmare spectacle. For if "The Babysitter" is playful, it also reveals the latent violence in our middle-class culture. Its importance derives from the realization of this violence in a form that brings everything into its own level, onto its dynamic and random surface. And it may be considered within an important if minor body of what Raymond Federman calls "surfiction,"[5] which presses the novel in motion to a limit and provides a vantage from which we can view its development.

CHAPTER NINE

Riding the Surf: Raymond Federman
Walter Abish, and Ronald Sukenick

Coover's "The Babysitter" may well have been influenced by
Alain Robbe-Grillet's *Jealousy*—which consists of a series of un-
linked present moments, where what happens includes what
might be imagined or invented, and where we can never get beyond the surface of the printed text. But the narrator, unlike his
counterpart in Coover's story, is not above and beyond the narrative. He is certainly beyond our grasp, for he never describes,
locates, or even alludes to himself, but he is completely within the
story. Though we never see him, we feel his presence in the ve-
randa chair set some distance apart from A . . . and Franck, or
watching them in the courtyard through a blemished windowpane. Moreover, everything we do see is his obsession: A . . .
combing her hair, writing a note, arranging the chairs, or talking
with Franck about their trip to town; the sound of the crickets; the
crouching of the native; the squashing of the centipede. The novel
is almost entirely descriptive, but each description—with its
obsessive attention to detail, its varied recurrences, and its
increasing sense of violence—becomes an event in the narrator's
consciousness. But we know nothing of the narrator. He never
tells us his relation to the characters or just why he is obsessed
with the events—indeed, he never even speaks in the first person.
All we know is each event as it comes into existence in the present
moment of narration. And the present moment of narration exists
only in the printed text—on the surface of the page, which, containing no dots or spaces, is absolutely full. It is absolutely all
there. And absolutely all there is.

Raymond Federman, Walter Abish, and Ronald Sukenick also
have been influenced by Robbe-Grillet and the French literary

movements he generated, the *nouveau roman* and the *tel quel.* Their novels maintain the obdurate presence of the printed text, where life and fiction intersect, but they also engage us in what becomes the dynamic of the novel's surface—the surf of their fictions. Although they run the risks of appearing superficial, they are indeed engaging. Moreover, they are important in that they press the novel in motion to its limits, providing perspective on its earlier manifestations but also discovering new territories of human consciousness.

"Surfiction"—a term invented by Raymond Federman—exposes man as irrational and life as a fiction. Federman refers not only to the fictional nature of contemporary reality but, following Robbe-Grillet, to the fact that such a fiction has no preestablished meaning. Events gain meaning only in their "recounted form," their "verbalized version." Nor does language *reproduce* a preexisting meaning: it *produces* meaning, creates meaning as it goes along, as it does its tricks.[1] It is just such a movement that Federman embodies in the striving of his narrative voices—which themselves arise from language doing its tricks on the printed page.

Take It or Leave It, as the subtitle proclaims, is "an exaggerated second-hand tale to be read aloud either standing or sitting."[2] To be read aloud is the key, for Federman has composed a novel of voices for voices—declaimers, singers, bellowers, mumblers, addicts of sound and rhythm, suffering subvocalizers. A Frenchman who has lived in America for thirty-five years and preserved an "incredible accent" while cultivating a marvelous ear for American speech and jazz rhythms, he also owes a debt to Rabelais and Beckett, who in opposite ways extended the tradition of the oral narrative into print.

To Rabelais he owes a verbal torrent that seems to take on a life of its own, embracing both the demotic and the erudite, and accumulating—in description, narration, peroration,and characterization—a gigantic vitality. *Take It or Leave It* also follows Rabelais in being a comic quest for knowledge, an episodic journey into the known and the unknown. The journey takes a young French-American paratrooper to Camp Drum in upper New York State in search of his back pay and identity papers. It takes him from the induction center where, to a volley of beerbelly laughs, he asks (with his incredible accent) what he was supposed to do to get into the Frogmen. It takes him to Fort Bragg where, as the "Cyrano of the Regiment," he writes love letters for all the guys in the barracks: "Fabulous dreams. Unbreakable vows of all types. Uncontrolled promises. Endless resolutions. Languishing memories. . . . Weeping descriptions of Nature in local colors. Wild erotic situations of surrealistic denseness whose filaria of suggestiveness was certainly enough to corrupt even the most perverse kinds of minds. Positions and contortions that would require for correct execution and proper results the acrobatic talents of the entire population of a zoo or tiergarten." And it takes him through the icy spaces of Vermont where his Buickspecial skids off the road and into "the salutory branches of that big beautiful Christmas tree well rooted at the bottom of the gully."

But the journey is intellectual as well as physical and goes back as well as forward in time: it explores the hero's past as well as his politics, philosophy, and aesthetics. The journey also explores the many ways of telling about the past and the present—and this leads us to another French writer if not a Frenchman who also extended the tradition of oral narrative into print. Samuel Beckett is the subject of Federman's critical study *Journey to Chaos*, and the voices in Federman's novel often address Sam and unashamedly steal ("play-giarize") from Beckett's voices. In plays like *Krapp's Last Tape, Happy Days, Play,* and *Not I,* and in novels like *Molloy, Malone Dies,* and *The Unnamable,* Beckett reduces his characters to voices. He dramatizes the plight, the energy, the inventiveness, the minor victories and major defeats of characters who are compelled to tell their stories and say their say. But whereas Beckett's voices, trapped in a language that is not theirs, agonize over the need to speak, Federman revels in this situation. He takes joy in the fact that he cannot separate himself from his fictions, is flushed by the need to go on, to invent, improvise, extend himself into the unknown through language.[3]

So many of Beckett's voices are alone, but Federman's main voice is always surrounded by noisy listeners. In fact, we never hear the principal voice directly. We hear it only though the mediating voice of a "secondhand teller" as he stands on a windy platform and tries to tell his tale to a group of listeners who continually interrupt, question, and harangue him. What we hear then (and we too are addressed among the listeners) is a tall tale told by a secondhand teller who often weaves the voice of his hero in with his own, as he argues with his interlocutors over the character of his hero, his motivation, his politics, as well as the mode of storytelling, the state of fiction, and the critics of fiction. The mediating voice of the secondhand storyteller magnifies the "told" or raises him toward an epic level by trying to tell about him over the voices of the listeners. And the mediating voice must go on, progress, create the "told" and the meaning of his story with words that are continually disputed or undermined. A major conflict, then, which competes with the conflicts in the storyline, is among the many voices in the novel. Or, to put it another way, the comic problem of mediation—of how the story gets to us and what keeps it from getting to us—is as engaging as the story itself.

What engages us, in fact, is not only the story and not only the voices but the story and the voices as they appear in the concrete language of the novel, or as they evolve from the blank page into the printed text. "All the characters and places in this book are real," we are told in the prefatory disclaimer, "they are made of words." The subject, as funny as it is, is always mediated by the voice of the secondhand teller; and his voice, as energetic and resourceful as it is, comes to us only through the medium of the printed words. Even the characters are made of words—are uniquely evoked by the novel's imaginative typography.

The typography, which I mention last though it engages us first, is the novel's medium and the novel's reality. Federman composes not by the sentence or even by the line but by the page—using a variety of typefaces and arranging the words in patterns that evoke a wide range of rhythms and conflicts as well as a visual experience that often engages us for its own sake. There is no way of representing the reality of *Take It or Leave It* because the reality is the entire novel continually evolving: concrete language, "doing its own tricks," creating voices, building momentum, going against the very obstacles it creates for itself, dallying with familiar forms but continually giving birth to itself, enlarging itself—and enlarging the consciousness of its reader.

Take It or Leave It is all voices, though they are made of words, as they are shaped on the surface of the page and build momentum. Walter Abish's *Alphabetical Africa* has no voice. The narrative is brought to life—a continent is created, populated with characters, and animated by events—through the regular accretion of letters. "Ages ago, Alex, Allen and Alva arrived at Antibes, and Alva allowing all, allowing anyone, against Alex's admonitions and Allen's angry assertion. . . . "[4] It is not a narrative voice but the letter "a" that sets the novel in motion—establishes a past, creates three characters, distinguishes their characteristics, and brings them to a continent that fills up with ants, antelopes, alligators, and angular Africans whom attractive Alva arouses. She also arouses the "author's analytically aggressive anticipations again and again" (1). Thus the continent comes to include the author, who writes a novel in his suburban home, an African map on its garage wall, travels to Africa, and even gives Alva pages of his manuscript for comment. It also includes the events of language reaching its limits, mocking itself, and creating new possibilities. When the "author assumes Alva's asexuality affected African army's ack-ack accuracy" (2), the language strains under the enforced alliteration as well as the effect of an onomatopoetic euphemism, and contracts a speech defect.[5]

The universe of *Alphabetical Africa* expands even more as we move from chapter to chapter, for each new chapter admits words beginning with another letter. In the first chapter every word begins with "a"; hence the characters and events, though singularly individualized by the arbitrariness of form, are limited. In the second chapter words begin with "a" and "b"; the third chapter, "a," "b," and "c"; and so on. The characters therefore develop new traits (Alex and Allen become killers), their stories take new turns (they hunt Alva), and a great many new characters and story lines are set in motion by the alphabetical evolution. New possibilities emerge, and the story becomes richer because more words—and more grammatical alternatives—become available. In the "h" chapter a character may become a "he," and we are surprised to discover how much new space and flexibility is created by this common pronoun—it is as if we were discovering a new territory. In the "i" chapter the author takes on a new dimension: "I haven't been here before." In the "n" chapter he can invoke a "now"—creating an ambiguous temporal dimension by refering to both the now of the story and the now of his composing it. In the "y" chapter the universe of the novel comes to include "you" and the reader is drawn in.

Yet while narrative movement from "a" to "z" causes the novel's universe to expand, it also causes Africa to shrink. The continent fills up with words, and the words bridge what, due to lexical limitations, were actual gaps. The author discovers not only the creative but the destructive potential of language as it evolves: "If Africa is really shrinking it'll be more difficult for Alva to evade Alex and Allen. And both are persistent" (56). Moreover, he discovers the imperialistic tendency of Western language as it intrudes upon the unknown and consolidates diversity. In the "b" chapter Alex and Allen bribe a building attendant; in the "c" chapter colonialists arrive; in the "h" chapter "dictionaries

hamper black farmers" (17). Alva, though she is being hunted by
Alex and Allen, is pursuing her own course, seductively distract-
ing Africans from Africa's shrinkage. "However, a few letters are
still missing, consequently a few prime ministers are still not
listed in her appointment book" (50). When the Queen holds a
news conference, it upsets the author. All the empty spaces are
disappearing: "vanishing Africa, vanishing Alva, vanishing
African armies . . . " (57).

The second half of the novel moves from "z" to "a," and while
the lexical possibilities decrease, we are drawn on by what the author can make happen in his diminishing space. In the end Alex,
Allen, and Alva are leaving Africa—but Alphabetical Africa remains, a complete world. Even as the letters vanish, the language
has done its work. The empty spaces of the early chapters cannot
be restored. The language, developing and diminishing with mechanical regularity, has become a creative reality and a totalizing
force.

Surfiction, as we have seen in *Take It or Leave It* and *Alphabetical Africa*, evokes a world that is all surface, or all surf—encom-
passing facts of contemporary reality and fictions that are not so
discernible from facts, events that are possible and events made
possible by the power of language, the author's actualities, actual
inventions, and actual act of composition. Federman generates
the ebullience of his surf through imaginative typography. Abish
generates a creative and destructive power by giving in to alphabetical sequence. Ronald Sukenick creates a surf that lacks their
scope and richness because its substance continually gives way to
its motion. But he pushes the novel in motion to its limit, and he
creates an experience of motion that has singular power. Like
Hawthorne's wandering Jew and Melville's confidence man,
Sukenick is an outlaw and trickster who reveals a world where
senseless movement is all there is, draws us in, and compels us to
take responsibility for it.

Ronald Sukenick: Brooklyn boy in cowboy boots. Wanted for
"Death of the Novel." For growing *Up*. For running *Out*. For
counterfeiting the normalcy of *98.6*.[6]

Ronald Sukenick: Hawthorne's wandering Jew, returned with
interest—traveling with a diorama on his back, inviting us to look
through its orifices, exhibiting a series of outrageous scratchings
as specimens of art. The pictures are blurred, for they are in constant motion and replace one another with haphazard swiftness.
In their midst is often seen a gigantic, brown, hairy hand—which

might be mistaken for the Hand of Destiny, though in truth it is only the showman's—pointing its forefinger to various scenes of conflict, while its owner gives historical illustrations.[7]

Ronald Sukenick: confidence man. Ronnie to his wife. Professor Sukenick to his libidinous student as well as his fifteen-year-old mistress. Mr. Suchanitch to his department chairman Whitebread Blackhead. Rex to the reader opening *Out*, before turning into Carl, Donald, Harrold, then Carl again dreaming he's Henry Aldrich. Ron inviting the children of Frankenstein to form a commune so that he can write *98.6* without inventing characters, and also Tante Goldie's good boy ("If you'll promise to stop crying," says the Israeli prime minister, "I'll tell you a few things"— about Einstein" [186]).

Ronald Sukenick: exploiter of women, sadist, guru, quick-change artist, juggler, one-man band, master of the shell game, satanic creator who thrives on destruction and deconstruction, descendant of the trickster god Hermes, fleet-footed surfer.

As noted earlier, surfiction, according to Raymond Federman, exposes man as irrational and reality as a fiction.[8] It also exposes the world as all surface, or all surf. Hawthorne's wandering Jew and Melville's confidence man revealed the dark underside of the daylight world and the reality beneath man's fictions; the surfictionist reveals a world that has no underside—where the surface is all there is, where what actually happens is indistinguishable from fiction, and where fiction actually happens.

Sukenick, the protagonist of *Up*, is initiated into his first job, in the maternity ward of a city hospital, while back home his uncle is dying. He carries a stillbirth—a giant baby in a shoe box—to the morgue. But it is returned, so he takes it to the lab.

> "I can't take this."
> "Why not?"
> "It's too old. I can't take no cadaver. This here is a cadaver. This goes to the morgue."
> "The morgue just sent it back."
> "What do you mean? They got to take it. This is a cadaver."
> He closes the box. I pick up the cadaver and we both go over to the morgue. The guy in the morgue is a prick from the word go. A sharp type who looked like a bookie, and very up on what was his job and what was yours.
> "It ain't a cadaver," he insists. "It's a fetus."
> "That's no fetus—it's all developed," says the guy from the lab.
> "If it's a cadaver where's its death certificate?"
> "It don't have a death certificate," I say.
> "Then as far as I know it's still alive. Take it away."

"It's not alive," says the guy from the lab. "It don't have a birth
certificate. It was never born."

"In that case it don't exist," says the guy from the morgue.

(74–75)

In such a world fiction does not imitate life; therefore such well-
established canons as the imitative and intentional fallacy are
fallacious. All canons, hierarchies, purposes, and meanings are
called into question. Or, as Sukenick argues: "Reality doesn't
exist, time doesn't exist, personality doesn't exist. God was the
omniscient author, but he died; now no one knows the plot."[9]
Everything has been leveled, but everything is on the level. After
a relatively conventional *Up*, Sukenick's confidence man contributes to the leveling. Everything is there, on the page, where the
author, his characters, his story, their stories, fragments of the
contemporary world, figments of the imagination, and the text
itself—all equally responsible and irresponsible—create the
surf and ride it. The surf, exhilarating and threatening its riders
as it challenges their skill and cunning, is in constant motion.
Sukenick makes the motion itself the subject of *Out* and *98.6*.

"This is the start of a journey," says the protagonist of *Out*. "I
don't know how long it will be or where it takes you no one ever
does. All you do is keep track" (11). The journey, impossible or
purposeless, across expanses of empty space, is archetypically
American. Thoreau dignifies the "saunterer" by inventing his
etymology and tracing him back to the "idle people who roved
about the country in the Middle Ages . . . under the pretense of
going *à la Sainte-Terre*," to the Holy Land.[10] Melville's Moby Dick
and Faulkner's Old Ben realize their power and mystery from
their ceaseless, indeterminate motion, which Ahab and Ike try to
constrain. Huckleberry Finn must light out for the territory.
Whitman celebrates "Nature without check" and expresses it in
the unchartable movement of "Song of Myself," and Henry
Adams gives ambiguous testimony to its manifestation in the dynamo. Senseless movement dominates the novels of Dos Passos,
Hemingway, Fitzgerald. Kerouac inspired a generation with *On
the Road*. But it took Pynchon to reveal the demonic power of
movement for its own sake, recalling Melville in the confidence
woman of *V.*, and realizing this movement not only in his subject
but in the dynamic structure of his novel. In *Out* Sukenick confronts the reader even more directly with this movement.

"Don't fall. Each of us carries a stick of dynamite. Concealed on
his person. That does several things. One it forms a bond. Two it

makes you feel special. Three it's a mute articulation of the conditions we live in. . . . This is your stick. Don't fall. We know one among us is a government agent that's inevitabe. Maybe it's you. Maybe it's me. . . . You're either part of the plot or part of the counterplot" (1). Sukenick's confidence man, addressing the reader in the second person, draws us into a world where everything is senselessly connected, or part of a senseless plot. Even more, he reduces the world of the sixties to sheer plot—that is, conspiracy and movement from event to event without agents, goals, or ends. And finally, without ending, he empties the world of all content, drawing the reader into empty space.

The movement of the novel, besides following what turns out to be a journey from the east to the west coast, takes two forms. The first is in the characters, who, not trusting anyone, have aliases, change names, and continually meet characters with their names. Rex and Ova introduce themselves as Carl and Velma to the junkie who, after robbing them on the stairway, assaults them in the courtyard ("Oh shid sorry. You can't see a funkin thing down here. Shid you oughta stay outa these dark courtyards they're dangerous" [14]) and offers them some of their money back. They remain Carl and Velma as the plot develops, at least for eight pages, until Carl meets the agent who introduces himself as Carl, and then Carl becomes Donald. When the agent Carl takes Donald home, he introduces him to Ova, who now has auburn hair. After Donald becomes Harrold and then Nick, he meets a man who insists that Nick is Carl, for he himself is Nick and never gets names wrong.

The second and more essential form of movement is in the very form of the novel, which drives the reader to read faster and faster. The reader is told that he too carries a stick of dynamite and "the countdown starts with nine" (4). What this means is that the second chapter is headed 9, then 8,7,6,5,4,3,2,1. The reader's momentum increases because each chapter has successively less print and more space—chapter 9 is composed of nine-line blocks separated by one line of space, chapter 8 of eight-line blocks with two lines of space, and so on down to chapter 1 where each line is separated by nine lines of space. Compelled more by the violent momentum than by the violence of the story, the reader leaps across more and more space; and the momentum increases as some sentences run on without punctuation within a block and some sentences complete themselves across a space. Due to Sukenick's fine ear for the idiom and mastery of the printed line, we are able to

keep on the track. We read faster and faster across more and more
space until there is

> . . . no more leeway 987654321 wake up
> this way this way this way this way this way this way this
> way out this
> way out
> 0
> [in the center of the last printed page]

And finally eleven pages of empty space.

After riding the swift surf of the novel, the reader is swept *out*.
The novel and the reader are emptied of all words and all thought.
Now—fully awakened and moving on his own—the reader continues into the empty space, facing nothing. Or facing what Sukenick describes in his next novel as "the gap. The blank space the
clean slate. Where the terror is. And where dreams condense like
clouds in an empty sky" (171).

While *Out* moves westward to the open sea, *98.6* moves east-
ward to the hol(e)y land. "Who knows what salvations we might
pluck from circumstance if we were open to the unknown" (168).
The novel begins with a plucking from circumstance, moves
through a period of being plucked by circumstance, and ends with
the salvation of wholeness in the holey land. "Frankenstein," the
first part, is a series of disordered and discontinuous diary entries,
plucked from the past of an anonymous third person. It counter-
points a journey across a sea and through a desert to the Ancient
Caja with a return to his country "racing like a wheel" (9). The
second section, "Children of Frankenstein," turns into a continuous third-person narrative describing the formation and dissolution of a commune in California. Dissolution is inevitable because
the commune cannot withstand the pressures from without—the
law, the anarchist hippies, and the terrorist motorcycle gang. Dissolution is also inevitable because of its members' natural impulse
toward violence. But, more important, it is inevitable because its
seeds are sown in the very act of forming: in its rejection of society's norms but also in its construction of the building that they
call "The Monster":

> following the suggestions in fact the capabilities of the materials.
> . . . Plus everybody getting in on the design like Joan getting obses-
> sed with geodesic domes and George with the tower and Ron with tele-
> scoping lateral extensions off one side of the foundation and Joan get-
> ting off into multiplying intricacies of a single corner which turns out
> to be the only corner because Ralph puts his heart into avoiding all

angles in the ground plan and Evelyn insists on irregular windows and doors like in Arab buildings she says. (66)

In the end the dissolution is reflected in the very language that Ron is using to write a novel about the commune.

> He recognized The Missing Lunk on the last S & D Mission. He heard it coming out of Lance's mouth. That is what he heard was not The Lunk but the fact that it was Missing. That's when he decided to speak the kind of language people don't understand. If they don't understand it The Lunk can hide there. As soon as they understand it they hunt it down and then The Lunk is Missing again. At the first sign of a lurking Lunk they send out S & D Missions all over the place. This language that people don't understand is extremely stupid and nonsensical and is the language The Lunk speaks. (161)

But the language, which continues nonsensically and poetically to the end of the chapter, is also a new beginning, or a new opening to the unknown. "Palestine," the final section, is a short, fast, first-person monologue set in Israel (Is-real). Israel is the holey land and the promised land. It is holey with the promise of wholeness, for it continues the kibbutz or ideal commune; indeed, it contains the kibbutz where surfing is practiced, giving "every man and woman direct access to that union with nature so sought after by the sages" (172). It also contains the wise Arab Yitzak Fawzi, with his mystical knowledge of particles and waves, and the wise Jew Golda Meir, who has been tutored by Einstein and Buber.

The disordered and discontinuous diary entries of "Frankenstein," the third-person narrative of "Children of Frankenstein," and the language of The Missing Lunk are finally brought together in "Palestine." We finally become attuned to the Mosaic Law— "the law of mosaics or how to deal with parts in the absence of wholes" (167). And we finally become attuned to the voice and consciousness of the novel—plucking salvation from circumstance as it reaches into the unknown, constantly moving forward as it attempts to embrace the parts and the holes, the facts of the past and present, personal recollections and reactions, imagined fears and possibilities. It also reaches for wholeness in the holey land, attempting to see, grasp, and say everything at the same time, like Jesse Lone Cat Fuller, the one-man band:

> playing all the instruments AT THE SAME TIME I'm sitting in Laguna Beach with the cat on my lap listening to The San Francisco Blues by Lone Cat Fuller AT THE SAME TIME trying to finish my novel AT THE SAME TIME trying to forget about it I pick and open a

book at random Fuller Buckminster quotes Fuller Margaret all attempts to construct a national literature must end in abortions like the monster of Frankenstein things with forms but soulless and therefore revolting we cannot have expression till there is something to be expressed AT THE SAME TIME trying to forget about it a trip a bar in a distant city turns out to be called Frankenstein franks and steins AT THE SAME TIME this morning's mail with an article by Ihab Hassan on Prometheus Frankenstein Orpheus AT THE SAME TIME thinking when you try to sew Orpheus back together what you get is Frankenstein AT THE SAME TIME hearing on the radio Lon Chaney just died a few miles away from here in San Clemente AT THE SAME TIME reading this record jacket thinking yes ramble around settle in California pick up this and that adapt it to your style without sidemen the novelist is a one man band playing all the instruments AT THE SAME TIME playing along on a kazoo AT THE SAME TIME moving to San Francisco AT THE SAME TIME entering the State of Israel AT THE SAME TIME orchestrating the whole thing toward those Moments of Luminous Coincidence when everything comes together AT THE SAME TIME AT THE SAME TIME sorry to leave Southern California the sun the waves the mother tongue another bungled paradise AT THE SAME TIME happy to be heading for San Francisco another chance AT THE SAME TIME tying up my novel AT THE SAME TIME my life is unravelling AT THE SAME TIME the novel is bungled fragments stitched together AT THE SAME TIME everything is seamless perfect not because because because but AT THE SAME TIME playing the blues letting it go it is as it is. Another failure. (187–88)

Out is an experience of emptying. *98.6* is an experience of collecting. Both are novels of pure motion—of language on the printed page moving forward, creating and destroying, creating in its own destructions, fashioning connections out of its disconnections, carrying the known into the unknown. In *Out* the unknown is empty space or nothing. In *98.6* it is everything at the same time. If the empty space at the end of *Out* contains infinite possibility and infinite terror, so does the wholeness that climaxes *98.6* for it contains the holes. The holy land contains the chamber of horrors—a memorial to the concentration camps. It also contains Dr. Frankenstein, "whose researches have unlocked the secrets of life itself," who "has taught us how to create ourselves in finer and finer harmony with the rhythms of the cosmos," and who may be planning to "promote the kind of neoindustrialism with which [he is] identified in Europe and America" (172,183). Moreover, the movement of *98.6* has an ambiguous direction. It moves to the holy land, which houses the Ancient Caja. But we should remember that in the beginning of the novel, the protagonist had traveled across a sea and through a desert to see the

Ancient Caja before returning home—that is, "Palestine" may lead to "Frankenstein."

Sukenick's confidence man has created or exposed the surf of modern experience—the continually changing surface, which includes fact and fiction; historical events, imaginative events, and events on the printed page; the author, his characters, and his readers. He rides the surf with skill and cunning, drawing us in with him till we see and feel the movement of the surf as all there is.

CHAPTER TEN

Bring Back That Line, Bring Back That Time

This is not to say that surfiction is the ultimate mode of modern narrative, or that it realizes the fullest potential of the novel in motion. No matter what new sensations are generated, no matter what new territories of consciousness are opened, the novel yields less the more it reduces experience to a single plane. The surf of Federman's fiction is thick with texture, which includes a wide range of allusions, a rich sense of humor, and the excitement of battling against traditional expectations. In Abish the language is a creative force rising, as it were, beyond the page as it compels us to make—and judge—connections between what we are reading and what we know or thought we knew about modern history, which, we discover, includes the power of Western language. But Sukenick, while generating a singular experience of motion and realizing its sensations of terror and exhilaration, sacrifices texture and traps us in an intelligent and wily but nonetheless limited consciousness. The experience of his achievement recalls the problem Faulkner encountered in *Pylon*, which (as I pointed out in the Introduction) extends the senseless motion of airplane races into the very texture of his novel but fails to realize the power of his later novels just because it lacks their richness.

Still, surfiction, especially as it develops in Sukenick, does carry the novel in motion to a limit. It does embody in its purest state the creative and destructive force that has dominated modern consciousness, and it may lead us toward a new perspective on the earlier achievements of modern fiction. From this perspective, we might reassess our judgment of *Pylon*; but, more important, we might reassess just what it was we thought were modern fiction's major achievements. We may even look back to see whether we have developed the best way to read modern fiction and realize its full value.

The modernist revolution has been seen as a rejection of restrictive causality and oppressive linearity as embodied in the traditional plot line and inherent in the traditional point of view and mode of characterization. Indeed, I have emphasized the fragmentation, shifting perspectives, dislocations, discontinuities, unpredictable transformations, kaleidoscopic simultaneity, and leveling that generate the experience of uncontrolled and uncontrollable motion. But what has replaced temporal linearity has been described by Virginia Woolf as a "transparent envelope," by James Joyce as a mosaic, by Ezra Pound as "an intellectual and emotional complex in an instant of time," and by Joseph Frank in his enormously influential essay as "spatial form."[1] We have been led to read modern fiction to discover geometrical patterns that abrogate time, undermine authority, and liberate us from the inexorable plot line. If we reexamine this model from the perspective we have gained on the novel in motion, though, we will arrive at a description of the modernist revolution at once more conservative and more radical. We will restore a vital and major dimension of the reading experience that has been suppressed in the name of the modernist revolution. And we will discover that this very dimension is what generates the experience of terrifying but exhilarating movement from the known into the unknown.

SPACE HAS ITS LIMITS

As modernists and postmodernists, we are conspirators, accomplices, agents in the demolition of linearity. We take demonic joy in tearing up the track: in deconstructing the plot, in insisting that what happens next is not as important or as exciting as those patterns that abrogate time and are fashioned in terms of space. Our joy derives both from the Romantic urge to undermine causal necessity (like Dostoyevsky's underground man, we must prove that we are not piano keys) and from the discovery of new possibilities in literature and human consciousness. Lessing to the contrary, writers can evoke simultaneity; sequence can yield to juxtaposition; the narrative line can turn into a circle or mobile. Joseph Frank's essay on spatial form is as persuasive today as it was in 1945. Sharon Spencer's concept of architectonics illuminates some of the most engaging novels of the twentieth century.[2] We have even discovered new dimensions in traditional literature.

But the model of spatial form has suppressed a dimension that is found in the rudimentary sequence of events and in the movement from beginning to end. Even in a plotless work the reader encounters one image, idea, event after another and experiences their forward movement; and a subsequent reading follows the event of the first. Even in a circular text the end is different from the beginning, since it trails the sequence of events and is pressed into existence by their forward movement. Even when the writer strives for simultaneity, the reader experiences sequence. In each case the primary effect and meaning derive from the movement of a unique succession.

WHERE THE READER DRAWS THE LINE

"Everything should sound simultaneously," says Flaubert of the county fair scene in *Madame Bovary.* "One should hear the bellowing of the cattle, the whispering of the lovers, and the rhetoric of the officials all at the same time." According to Joseph Frank, Flaubert achieves simultaneity by halting the narrative's time flow and "cutting back and forth" between three spatial levels. On the street the mob mixes with the livestock, on the platform officials declaim bombastic platitudes, and upstairs in the town hall Rodolphe courts Emma with a rhetoric not too different from that of the officials. At the climax "Rodolphe's Chateaubriandesque phrases are read at almost the same moment as the names of prize winners for raising the best pigs."[3] But does the crosscutting really achieve simultaneity? Does the comic effect come from our hearing Rodolphe and the president at almost the same time? Or does the scene depend foremost on the sequence of phrases and gestures—and on Flaubert's genius for timing?

> "Take us, for instance," [Rodolphe] said, "how did we happen to meet? What chance willed it? It was because across infinite distances, like two streams uniting, our particular inclinations pushed us toward one another."
> And he seized her hand; she did not withdraw it.
> "First prize for general farming!" announced the president.[4]

Crosscutting is a term aptly borrowed from film—a medium that achieved an immediate and universal attraction through its capacity for movement. Indeed, crosscutting is one of the primary means of realizing this capacity. As I have pointed out, both Griffith and Eisenstein recognized how Dickens heightened suspense by crosscutting—as in *Oliver Twist* when he cut back and forth between the capture of Oliver and the old man waiting with his watch. By accelerating the crosscuts and shooting from more radical angles, Griffith and Eisenstein both heightened the suspense and increased the tempo in their chase scenes—in Griffith's last-minute rescues and in sequences like that on the Odessa Steps, where the hysterical crowd is chased by the orderly soldiers. Increased tempo and suspense are the most immediate effect of crosscutting, whether for the melodramatic purpose of the chase or the comic purpose of Flaubert's county fair. Simultaneity is a secondary effect, resulting from a quickly learned convention—although not so quickly learned as to preclude the apprehension expressed by Griffith's employers when he first proposed one.

When we speak of simultaneous dialogue in Flaubert, we are referring to a convention and to a metaphor. The same holds true for Pound's juxtaposition of images. Even in his famous example of an "intellectual and emotional complex in an instant of time," simultaneity is preceded by an experience of temporal succession and forward movement, and juxtaposition follows from a sequence that—no matter how illogical—is still linear:

In the Station of the Metro

The apparition of these faces in the crowd;
Petals on a wet, black bough.

The sequence of these lines—which includes the title—cannot be changed. The faces in the crowd are defined by the fact that the poet is in a Metro station, and the effect of the poem comes from our seeing the petals *after* the faces—just as the effect of Flaubert's passage comes from our hearing the president's announcement *after* hearing Rodolphe's speech on fate and seeing the couple join hands.

"Spatial form" is an evocative metaphor. It helped generate a new set of expectations and expand our reading habits, but taken literally it becomes misleading. Pound contributed to the critical confusion by heralding the Chinese ideograph, where simple images could be combined and presented simultaneously as a complex picture.[5] Other writers and critics, influenced by cubist painting, compounded the confusion by adding the metaphor of "collage" to our critical lexicon. Except for the short "concrete" poem, where units can be apprehended at a glance, Western literature demands to be read sequentially. Even when surfiction writers break up the page with parallel columns or other patterns that undermine our reading habits, we read in patterns that are sequential. Yet, as I tried to show in the early chapters, modernist literature is visual in a way that earlier literature rarely approached, and primarily because of the influence of modern painting. Writers have evoked experiences of simultaneity and multiple perspective. Novelists and playwrights have done away with the plot and have even turned the narrative line into a circle. Let me show how the narrative picture, even when fragmented or static, is dominated by a continuous forward movement; how multiple perspective in a timeless moment still yields a sequential scene; and how the circular plot is nonetheless linear. Then I will propose a model of temporal rather than spatial form that describes the modernist and postmodernist subversions of narrative time while preserving the major dimension of the reading experience and illuminating the singularly temporal dynamic of modern fiction.

REALIGNING THE FRAGMENTED PICTURE

In his essay on Dickens and Griffith, Eisenstein shows how the novelist captures the essence of Mr. Dombey in a remarkable description that fractures the normal, logical sequence of visual details.

> He had already laid his hand upon the bell-rope to convey his usual summons to Richards, when his eye fell upon a writing-desk, belonging to his deceased wife, which had been taken, among other things, from a cabinet in her chamber. It was not the first time that his eye had lighted on it. He carried the key in his pocket; and he brought it to his table and opened it now—having previously locked the room door— with a well-accustomed hand.

The last sentence, Eisenstein comments, "arrests one's attention" with its apparent awkwardness. The phrase *having previously locked the room door* is " 'fitted in' as if recollected by the author in the middle of a later phrase, instead of being placed where it apparently should have been, in the consecutive order of the description, that is, before the words, *and he brought it to his table.*" Dickens's choice was not fortuitous. "In this deliberate 'montage' displacement of the time-continuity of the description there is a brilliantly caught rendering of the *transient thievery* of the action, slipped between the preliminary action and the act of reading another's letter, carried out with absolute 'correctness' of gentlemanly dignity which Mr. Dombey knows how to give to any behavior or action of his."[6] By fragmenting the narrative picture, Dickens causes us to see Mr. Dombey in surprising depth; but, as Eisenstein implies, what we see is even more the result of the new, surprising, and successfully calculated sequence.

"My task which I am trying to achieve," wrote Joseph Conrad in words that D. W. Griffith would repeat ten years later and that might be used as an epigraph to modernism, "is, by the power of the written word to make you hear, to make you feel—it is, before all, to make you *see.*" *The Nigger of the Narcissus,* to which this declaration is prefaced, opens with a narrative picture that makes us see—indeed, engages us in the act of excited perception— through its fragmentation. Here the fragmentation is achieved not by breaking into the line of action but, as I have shown in chapter two, by a flashing of the narrative eye from one part of the ship to another, cutting back and forth in time, as well as from one close-up to another. My shot-by-shot analysis shows how the fragmentation is achieved by a *succession* of sharp changes in focus—and how the *successive* movements of the narrative eye, even more than the bustling activity, impart such vitality to Conrad's picture.

In contrast to Conrad's, Joyce's picture of E— C— and her companions contains very little movement. Boots prattle, mouths and eyes move gently, umbrellas are closed. But the narrative eye, flashing from point to point and fragmenting the scene more radically, competes with the subject for our attention. And in Faulkner's description of Dilsey, in the most static scene in *The Sound and the Fury,* the movement of the narrative eye overwhelms the subject. The narrator—trying to apprehend, comprehend, hold on to an experience that is both outrageous and awesome—shifts his focus so rapidly and fragments Dilsey so radically that she becomes almost unrecognizable.

In each case the movement of the narrative eye is irregular and unpredictable as it shifts its vantage and fragments the whole. But the narrative eye moves and refocuses successively, and we encounter one detail after another. This becomes strikingly clear when we transcribe such narrative pictures into shot-by-shot film scenarios. Indeed, the justification for these transcriptions is the sequential nature of both mediums. Therefore, no matter now erratic the scanning in space, one pictorial event succeeds another in time, creating the primary dynamic of both film and the reading experience.

REALIGNING THE FRACTURED SCENE

"What a lark! What a plunge!"[7] Virginia Woolf's Mrs. Dalloway has plunged into the morning air. She has also plunged from London of 1923 to Bourton of 1891. Her thoughts as well as her body in continual motion, she has walked across Victoria Street, through

the park, and along Bond Street—thinking of tonight's party, recalling her girlhood at Bourton, meeting an old Bourton friend,
looking in the store windows, thinking of her daughter and of her
tutor, the poor, embittered Miss Kilman, who has aroused a "brutal monster" of hatred within her. She pushes through the swing-
ing doors of Mulberry's florist. As she goes from jar to jar with
Miss Pym, "choosing nonsense . . . this beauty, this scent, this
colour," the experience and Miss Pym's affection are like a "wave
which she let flow over her and surmount that hatred, that monster." Suddenly there is the violent backfire of a motor car. Startled, she and Miss Pym go to the window. Now time is arrested,
and we are given a bird's-eye view—a multiple perspective from
somewhere above the scene—of the general reaction, which includes the reaction of Mrs. Dalloway seen from the outside. Pas-
sersby stop and stare. A male hand draws the blind on the auto
window. Rumors circulate. Edgar J. Watkiss anounces, "The
Proime Minister's kyar." Mrs. Dalloway comes to the window
"with her arms full of sweet peas." Lucrezia Smith wonders if it is
the queen going shopping. Septimus Smith—having thought
"some horror had come almost to the surface and was about to
burst into flames"—declares that he will kill himself.

But when Clarissa emerges from the shop wearing "a look of extreme dignity," we realize that a great deal has happened during
this arrested moment—and we see much more in Mrs. Dalloway
than we did when she entered. That is, while time was arrested
and we saw what was happening simultaneously in different
places, a sequence of events was building to a climax.

The "brutal monster" stirring in Clarissa's breast was her hatred of Miss Kilman, who was "one of those spectres with which
one battles in the night." What she hated was the puritanic seriousness and honesty, which caused Miss Kilman to be dismissed
from her school during the war. This seriousness highlights the
"nonsense" of Clarissa's life and—like the thought of Mrs. Fox-
croft still "eating her heart out because that nice boy was killed"
in the war—darkens Clarissa's day. Turning to the flowers, she
suppresses the "brutal monster." The backfire—in those days
when cars were few—startles her. But the backfire is more than a
social disturbance: it is a "pistol shot," a "violent explosion," and
it causes a violent shift in perspective. The motor car, with its
blind drawn by an anonymous hand, is ominous. Yet all of the reactions, including Clarissa's coming to the window with her arms
full of sweet peas, are oblivious to the threats. All except for Sep-

timus's, which brings forth a note of terror—recalling the reality of a war experience not long past, and giving resonance to what had been incongruous epithets characterizing the backfire, a "pistol shot," a "violent explosion." This terror had been kept barely beneath the surface by Mrs. Dalloway as she put its stimuli in their social place, turned back to her girlhood and forward to her party. Now, more fully realized in the mind of the reader, it is suppressed again as she identifies with the occupant of the motor car, whom she too thinks is the queen, and steps out into the public eye wearing "a look of extreme dignity."

Septimus's reaction is a new and unexpected event in the sequence of events captured in the arrested moment. It is tinged by the sequence of events leading up to it—on the one hand by the pastoral and social events with which it contrasts, and on the other by Clarissa's dark thoughts and the disproportionately warlike images of the backfire. His reaction also gives meaning to those earlier events, as does any climax of a sequence, retroactively changing their quality. It illuminates a dimension of terror we did not feel when they were first described, and also a dimension of Clarissa's consciousness far deeper than her social concerns and even her fear of aging. That Clarissa's mind remains beyond our view during the arrested moment, and that she emerges from the florist so much more fully characterized, attest to the power of the sequence —which, despite the arresting of time, is nonetheless temporal, and which dominates the reading experience. A second reading of the novel gives the scene even more meaning. This is partly because we can now go back and forth in the time of the novel and "spatially" relate Clarissa's brutal monster to Dr. Holmes, whom Septimus sees as a brute; because we can relate the impersonal and ominous motor car to that of Dr. Bradshaw, who is also impersonal and ominous; because Septimus does actually kill himself and Clarissa identifies with him. But even more so, the scene takes on a fuller meaning because the second reading follows the first, and the reader's experience develops in a new sequence.

"Life is not a series of gig lamps symmetrically arranged," says Virginia Woolf—meaning that human time is not a succession of equal, discrete, and static moments, and that the novelist should not be bound by the mechanics of the well-made plot. It is "a luminous halo, a semi-transparent envelope surrounding us from the beginning of consciousness to the end."[8] But her images of the halo or envelope do not do justice to the dynamic quality of her work, or that of Joyce or Faulkner, who convey the movement from moment to moment in a more complex consciousness than the traditional novelist could imagine. Their scenes are not like a series of gig lamps symmetrically arranged to illuminate a mechanically causal sequence, but they do portray a sequence and convey a powerful sense of sequentiality in the mind of the reader. What we may look for, then, is a way to describe this sequence, or temporality, that would preserve the dynamic quality of its elements. Before we do so, let us move from the picture and scene to the largest narrative element.

REALIGNING THE CIRCULAR PLOT

The most static experience and the most circular plot I can think of are contained in Samuel Beckett's *Play*, and since plot functions similarly in drama and fiction, let me use *Play* for its graphic exemplification. Throughout the entire forty minutes of this drama, we see three identical gray urns, about a yard high and touching one another. From each urn protrudes a head, facing "undeviatingly front" and looking "so lost to age and aspect as to seem almost part of [the] urn."[9] In the center is a man; on each side is a woman. Their speech is provoked by a sharply focused spot light, which turns on and off without any apparent design, most often spotting a single face but occasionally spotting all three and provoking a chorus of simultaneous but different lines. Although the urns touch, the characters are unaware of each other's presence and speak broken monologues. The gratuitous spotlight compels them to break into one another's monologue, sometimes in a way to maintain the narrative, sometimes in a way to confuse it. From separate points of view, each character recalls his or her relationship in the triangle, which remains agonizing even after the man leaves each woman thinking he is with the other. Then each character speaks of the present, which, though consciousness is kept painfully alive, is better than the past. After the final chorus the entire play is repeated.

There is no time in Beckett's hell; the unremitting spotlight keeps the past always present and maintains the agonizing isolation. The characters repeat their lines twice; and we are made to feel that they will continue repeating them. But when we hear the first woman begin for the second time—"I said to him, Give her up."—we only first understand her. We first understand her reference to the earthly triangle, since the relationship had only become clear halfway through the first recitation. Moreover, we first understand that he can never give her up, that none of the characters can give the others up. And when we hear the man's final line—"We were not long together."—the irony is quantitatively and qualitatively different from the irony we first experienced, for we have now known a segment of their time. And the "we" now includes us. Beckett's hell is timeless in that the characters' past is always present, and the present is always being repeated. But his hell does have duration—which is the key to *Play*. On the one hand, "duration" means "to last" and derives from the same root as "durance," which is "imprisonment." On the other hand, it is defined by Henri Bergson as "the continuous progress of the past which gnaws into the future and which swells as it advances."[10] Despite Beckett's circular plot—which creates an experience of lasting and being imprisoned forever in the same state of separate agony—the events as they occur and recur form a continuous line, each succeeding event being both old and new, swelling as it brings the past into the present, and looking forward to a new future.[11] Beckett gives Dante's motto singular power by dramatizing a circle of the inferno—but even more, by dramatizing the experience of time moving from the past through the present and into the future with absolutely no hope.

BRING BACK THAT LINE, BRING BACK THAT TIME

Pierre Menard "did not want to compose another *Don Quixote*—which would be easy—but *the Don Quixote*." To do so, Borges's character did not try to learn seventeenth-century Spanish, re-embrace the Catholic faith, or forget the three hundred years of European history and literature that followed Cervantes's accomplishment. Nor did he copy *Don Quixote* word for word. Rather he used each of Cervantes's words in Cervantes's sequence—but as a novelist of the twentieth century influenced by Coleridge, Poe, Baudelaire, Mallarmé, and Valéry. So that to read the Menard *Quixote* would be to read Cervantes's words with entirely new associations and within an entirely new context—a context including the event of the original. "This technique, with its infinite applications, urges us to run through the *Odyssey* as if it were written after the *Aeneid*" and "would fill the dullest books with adventure. Would not the attributing of *The Imitation of Christ* to Louis Ferdinand Céline or James Joyce be a sufficient renovation of its tenuous spiritual counsels?"[12]

Borges illuminates the temporal, sequential dynamic of the reading experience—which is heightened rather than suppressed as modern writers reject, deconstruct, transform, displace the time-line of the traditional plot. This is the line of continuous forward movement that—even more than the narrative time-line and often despite it—presses the past into the present and makes each event new. Borges makes us feel the movement of the past into the present by creating a dynamic line from the event of Cervantes's publication through three hundred years of European history, a line that culminates in an audacious and new creative act.

Writers and critics who rebelled against the well-made plot and discovered ways of abrogating the narrative time-line were reacting to the mechanization of a time-dominated consciousness—to quantification, uniformity, and causality, or the reduction of time into a series of discrete, identical, and irreducible moments, following one another in an inexorable sequence. Ironically, they were reacting to a spatial view of time based on the movement of clock hands, on the turning of calendar pages, on the time-governed conveyer belts that reduced products and people to replaceable parts, on the scientific measurements of time against distance on the lines of a coordinate graph.

Despite the temporal and kinetic impulses of impressionism, futurism, the movies, jazz, Henry Adams's heralding of the dynamo, Ezra Pound's call to "make it new," and recent experiences of "future shock," our literary critical consciousness is still shackled by the spatial metaphors of rational nineteenth-century thought. This is partly because critical terms are metaphors, and most metaphors are pictorial or spatial. There are metaphors, however, that are not spatial and that describe the modernist subversions of narrative time while preserving the temporal dynamic. Modern physicists have been singularly beset by the problem of pictorial or spatial metaphors as they have come to see time, and not space, as the primary element of the universe. Mileč Čapec points out that they now use the term "event" to define what were classically called "particles," or the primary elements of physical reality.[13] And we might well follow their example by seeing words, images, dialogues, ideas, and actions as events—thereby recognizing the temporal, linear dynamic that affects us more strongly than the story's actual time-line.[14] Indeed, we would be recognizing the events as they follow one another on the printed page as the actuality of fiction.

Čapec also provides a model for the physical universe—based on musical progression—that also illuminates the temporal, linear dynamic of narrative events. Every tone in a melody or polyphony is discrete and irreducible. But each tone is "tinged" by the sequence of prior tones and, retrospectively, changes the quality of the tones that formed the sequence.[15] Here we have a linearity that is not mechanical but organic, that is ultimately formed by not discrete but continuous elements, that retains the uniqueness of each element while maintaining their mutuality. Here we have a movement that, although not unidimensional, reaches forward to an end that is always different from the beginning, and that gives the sequence its effect and meaning. Two events may occur simultaneously, but as one follows another in the narrative dynamic, the second gives resonance and meaning to the first. The flashback—on the screen or in the stream of a character's consciousness—is always present for the first time, having swollen and changed with accumulated associations. There are no circular plots, for there are no repetitions of either acts or words. The second part of *Play* is different from the first. And Menard has written a new *Quixote*.

Despite their arguments or intentions, our best modern and postmodern writers have heightened the temporality of the reading experience by building a dynamic linearity into the very substance of their pictures, their scenes, and their plots—no matter how fragmented, timeless, or circular. Modern fiction begins with the urge to see, which is an urge toward immediacy—or a continuous engagement in the present that grows out of the past but also refigures it as it reaches into the future and becomes radically new. And as modern fiction develops, the experience of this movement becomes more immediate. When the narrator engages us in the act of excited perception, he compels us to discover not what *happened* but what is *happening*, not what he arranged for us but what is *there* in the *now* of his story. Eventually, what is *there* and what is *now* come to include the event of the story being told and formed on the printed page. Faulkner's narrator may be focusing on the past, but he catches us up in his present as he shifts from one perspective to another and weaves his voice in and out of his storytellers' voices, trying to grasp the senseless dynamic of what happened. The "ineluctable modality" of Joyce's medium in *Ulysses* becomes a gratuitous force, causing us to leap back and forth between modern and Homeric times, intruding between us and what happened to the characters, threatening them and us with its capricious presence. The narrative voice of Beckett's trilogy usurps the narrating characters, denying them their pasts as well as any assurance of their existence in the present; and we become engaged in their heroic effort to go on. Nabokov undermines our security with the gaps in his narrative, which draw us from the possibilities of what happened to the possibilities of what may happen. Pynchon leads us through a series of radical transformations, one moment succeeding another as in a quantum jump. Coover engages us in a kaleidoscopic spectacle that is both wide in compass and long in duration, and where the action goes in all directions at once. Federman, Abish, and ultimately Sukenick bring everything into the surf of their fiction until there is nothing but its movement—which is an experience of sheer temporality.

All these writers fracture and displace narrative time. But in their different ways they engage us in a narrative sequence that, far more than the traditional novelist's, is an experience of moving through time and history. And it is precisely in their exploitation of the traditional novel's most essential dimension—the rudimentary sequence of events and the movement from beginning to end—that they engage us in the most radical experiences of modern consciousness. They continually upset our equilibrium by generating sensations of dislocation, discontinuity, shifting perspectives, directionless motion, unpredictable transformation, and leveling. But they continually situate us in the moment when the past joins with the future, where what happens refigures what happened and leads from the known into the unknown. They engage us in a temporal and historical motion that is ungoverned, ungovernable, and threatening—but also full of possibilities. And by denying us the security of a frame as well as the stability of a center, they compel us to take full responsibility for our perceptions, sensations, and judgments.

Notes

INTRODUCTION

1. See my *"Pylon, Awake and Sing!* and the Apocalyptic Imagination of the 30's," *Criticism* 8 (Spring 1971): 131–41.

2. For an interesting account of perception, which has influenced E. H. Gombrich in his recent work, see James J. Gibson, *The Senses Considered as Perceptual Systems* (Boston: Houghton Mifflin, 1966).

3. Ulric Neisser, "The Processes of Vision," *Scientific American* 219 (September 1968): 212.

4. Joel Snyder, "Picturing Vision," *Critical Inquiry* 6 (Spring 1980): 499–526.

5. "Il n'y a plus de perspective," quoted in Sergei Eisenstein, "Synchronization of the Senses," in *Film Sense*, ed. and trans. Jay Leyda (New York: Harcourt, Brace & World, 1947), pp. 96–97.

CHAPTER ONE

1. Daniel Defoe, *Moll Flanders*, ed. G. A. Starr (London: Oxford University Press, 1971), p. 121.

2. Daniel Defoe, *Robinson Crusoe*, ed. J. Donald Crowley (London: Oxford University Press, 1972), p. 11.

3. Samuel Richardson, *Pamela*, ed. William M. Sale, Jr. (New York: W. W. Norton, 1958), p. 10.

4. Ibid., p. 116.

5. Henry Fielding, *Joseph Andrews*, ed. Martin Battestin (Middletown, Conn.: Wesleyan University Press, 1975), pp. 42–43.

6. Henry Fielding, *The History of Tom Jones, A Foundling*, ed. Fredson Bowers (Middletown, Conn.: Wesleyan University Press, 1975), pp. 42–43.

7. Laurence Sterne, *Tristram Shandy*, ed. Ian Watt (Boston: Houghton Mifflin, 1965), p. 14.

8. Roman Ingarden, *The Literary Work of Art: An Investigation on the Borderlines of Ontology, Logic, and Theory of Literature*, trans. George G. Grabowicz (Evanston, Ill.: Northwestern University Press, 1973), pp. 246–54.

9. Rudolph Arnheim, *Visual Thinking* (Berkeley: University of California Press, 1971), p. 71. See also Gibson, *The Senses Considered as Perceptual Systems*; Neisser, "The Processes of Vision"; and David Norton and Lawrence Stark, "Eye Movements and Visual Perception," *Scientific American* 224 (June 1971): 35–43.

10. Tobias Smollett, *Humphry Clinker*, ed. Lewis M. Knapp (London: Oxford University Press, 1966), pp. 89, 93.

11. Robert Alter, *Partial Magic: The Novel as a Self-Conscious Genre* (Berkeley: University of California Press, 1975), pp. 96–102.

12. Mrs. D. W. Griffith, *When the Movies Were Young* (New York: E. P. Dutton, 1925), p. 66.

13. Actually, Porter may have initiated these dynamics the year before, in *The Life of an American Fireman*, by cutting back and forth between the mother and baby in a burning room and the fireman climbing to the rescue. But there is a controversy about the original print, and *The Great Train Robbery* was a far more popular film.

14. Jack Ellis makes this point in *A History of Film* (Englewood Cliffs, N.J.: Prentice-Hall, 1979), p. 48.

15. James Monaco, *How to Read a Film: The Art, Technology, History and Theory of Film and Media* (New York: Oxford University Press, 1977). p. 236. Also see Ellis, p. 29, for a comparison of film and earlier melodrama.

16. Sergei Eisenstein, "Dickens, Griffith, and the Film Today," in *Film Form: Essays in Film Theory*, ed. and trans. Jay Leyda (New York: Harcourt, Brace & World, 1949), pp. 214–24.

17. Eisenstein, "Synchronization of the Senses," pp. 98–99.

CHAPTER TWO

1. Gustave Flaubert, *Madame Bovary*, trans. Francis Steegmuller (New York: Random House, 1947), pp. 16–17.

2. Alan Spiegel, *Fiction and the Camera Eye: Visual Consciousness in Film and the Modern Novel* (Charlottesville: University Press of Virginia, 1976), p. 20.

3. Emile Zola, *L'Assommoir*, trans. Atwood H. Townsend (New York: New American Library, 1962), p. 8.

4. E. H. Gombrich, *Art and Illusion: A Study in the Psychology of Pictorial Representation* (Princeton, N.J.: Princeton University Press, 1969), p. 172.

5. Norton and Stark, "Eye Movements and Visual Perception."

6. Joseph Conrad, *The Nigger of the Narcissus* (Garden City, N.Y.: Doubleday, 1914), pp. 17–19.

7. James Joyce, *A Portrait of the Artist as a Young Man* (New York: Viking, 1964), p. 10. Subsequent page references will appear in the text.

8. There is little to suggest the reason for the change in chapter 5, although Joyce did experience difficulties in completing it. It is interesting, however, that at the time of its composition he was experimenting with word associatons and discovering the leaps that this entailed. In his notebook for *Exiles* we find:

N.(B)– 12 Nov 1913

Garter: precious, Prezioso, Bodkin
music, palegreen,
bracelet, cream sweets,
lily of the valley,
convent garden (Galway)
sea

Rat: Sickness, disgust, poverty
cheese, woman's ear,
(child's ear?)

Dagger: heart, death, soldier,
war, band, judgment
King

(Page 17, in the Lockwood Memorial Library, Buffalo, New York; also in Padric Colum's edition of *Exiles* [New York: Viking, 1951].)

9. Alan Spiegel uses the term "adventitious detail" for this modern phenomenon in his *Fiction and the Camera Eye.*

10. Margaret Church in a paper read at the Fourth International James Joyce Symposium, Dublin, 1973. Professor Church's point is developed in her *Structure and Theme: "Don Quixote" to James Joyce* (Columbus: Ohio State University Press, 1983).

CHAPTER THREE

1. See Bruce F. Kawin, *Faulkner and Film* (New York: Frederick Ungar, 1977), which also has a good discussion of Faulkner's use of montage.

2. Joseph Blotner, *Faulkner: A Biography*, vol. 1 (New York: Random House, 1974), p. 772.

3. Erwin Panofsky, "Style and Medium in Motion Pictures," in *Film Theory and Criticism*, ed. Gerald Mast and Marshall Cohen (New York: Oxford University Press, 1979), pp. 243-63.

4. See Wylie Sypher, *Rococo to Cubism in Art and Literature* (New York: Random House, 1960), pp. 257-88.

5. William Faulkner, *Flags in the Dust* (New York: Random House, 1973). All quotations from Faulkner's novels will be taken from the latest Random House editions; page references will appear in the text.

6. For further discussion see my *"Pylon, Awake and Sing!* and the Apocalyptic Imagination of the 30's."

7. Jean Stein, "William Faulkner: An Interview," in *William Faulkner: Three Decades of Criticism*, ed. Frederick J. Hoffman and Olga J. Vickery (New York: Harcourt, Brace & World, 1960), p. 80.

8. Ibid., p. 73.

9. I would distinguish the hovering narrator from the narrated monologue, or *erlebte rede*, by the duality of perspective. In the narrated monologue the narrator intrudes grammatically to effect an easy transition between the character's thoughts and the movement of the story; the hovering narrator intrudes as a disturbed witness to the character's thoughts and to the story, who adds his perceptions and reactions to those of the character. For discussion of narrated monologue, see Dorrit Cohn, "Narrated Monologue: Definition of a Fictional Style," *Comparative Literature* 18 (Spring 1966): 97-112.

10. See my *Stages of the Clown: Perspectives on Modern Fiction from Dostoyevsky to Beckett* (Carbondale, Ill.: Southern Illinois University Press, 1970), pp. 47-66.

11. For an important discussion of the role of the community, see Joseph W. Reed, Jr., *Faulkner's Narrative* (New Haven, Conn.: Yale University Press, 1973), pp. 134 ff.

12. Blotner, 1:785.

CHAPTER FOUR

1. Frank Budgen, *James Joyce and the Making of Ulysses* (Bloomington, Ind.: Indiana University Press, 1967), p. 228.

2. James Joyce, *Ulysses*, (New York: Random House,1961), p. 5. Subsequent page references will appear in the text.

3. David Hayman, *Ulysses: The Mechanics of Meaning* (Englewood Cliffs, N. J.: Prentice-Hall, 1970), chap. 5. Hayman sees the "counterforce" as the product of a "nameless creative persona or 'arranger' . . . a figure who can be identified neither with the author nor with his narrators, but who exercises an increasing degree of overt control over his increasingly challenging materials" (p. 70). Without questioning his concept of the "arranger," which serves to illuminate the narrative strategy of *Ulysses*, I would suggest that in accounting for the novel's grotesque effect we see the "counterforce" less anthropomorphically.

4. Eisenstein, *Film Form*, p. 10.

5. Budgen, *James Joyce and the Making of Ulysses*; A. Walton Litz, *The Art of James Joyce: Method and Design in Ulysses and Finnegans Wake* (London: Oxford University Press, 1961).

6. *Film Form*, p. 38.

7. Ibid., p. 104.

8. Hugh Kenner's brilliant discussion of the offstage action in the scene with Molly and Blazes Boylan, which begins with the question of who moved the furniture, suggests another important caesura in the novel. With this omitted scene, as with the omitted scene where Bloom asks Molly to bring him breakfast in bed, the reader collides with a gap in the narrative, a negative element with a palpably dramatic thrust. This kind of collision is basic to the work of Samuel Beckett. See Hugh Kenner, "Molly's Masterstroke," *James Joyce Quarterly* 10 (Fall 1972): 19-28.

9. Samuel Beckett, *Watt* (New York: Grove Press, 1959), p. 8. Subsequent page references will appear in the text.

10. *Molloy,* in *Three Novels by Samuel Beckett* (New York: Grove Press, 1965), p. 7. Subsequent page references for all three novels will appear in the text.

11. I am indebted to Carlotta Smith and Jeanne Whitaker's article on ellipses in Flaubert's *Un Coeur simple*, to appear in *Language and Style.* Molloy's "it" would be called an "unanchored pronoun."

CHAPTER FIVE

1. I am borrowing the term "galaxy" from Marshall McLuhan, *The Gutenberg Galaxy: The Making of Typographic Man* (Toronto: University of Toronto Press, 1962), although focusing on different elements and establishing a different emphasis. McLuhan's work has been dismissed by scholars for its impulsiveness and popularization, but it is still provocative and seminal. For a more scholarly treatment, see the works of Walter J. Ong, especially his *Interfaces of the Word: Studies in the Evolution of Consciousness and Culture* (Ithaca, N.Y.: Cornell University Press, 1977), where he illuminates what he calls the new "noetic economy."

2. Hugh Kenner, *Samuel Beckett: A Critical Study* (Berkeley: University of California Press, 1968), p. 17.

3. Quoted in Ortega y Gasset, *Man and Crisis*, trans. Mildred Adams (New York: W. W. Norton, 1958), p. 14.

4. Ibid.

5. See my "Limits of Realism," *College English* 31 (January 1970): 335-43.

6. Actually Brunelleschi established the rules of linear perspective, but Alberti put them into print. Moreover, "the two men had different intents. Brunelleschi carried out his unprecedented demonstrations as technological feats, not as acts of artistic composition" (Samuel Y. Edgerton, Jr., *The Renaissance Discovery of Linear Perspective*[New York: Basic Books, 1975], p. 40). Edgerton makes a num-

ber of interesting points distinguishing the ordering principles of the Renaissance from those of the Middle Ages. He relates the order of perspective painting to the "tidy principles of mathematical order" that "tight-fisted, practical-minded businessmen . . . applied to their bank ledgers," calling our attention to the fact that the definitive treatise on double-entry bookkeeping was written by a friend of Alberti's, the mathematician Luca Pacioli (p. 39). He also illuminates the religious and metaphysical values inherent in Alberti's motivation: "His perspective construction was intended to copy no specific place. It provided a purely abstract realm which the viewer would discern as a world of order: not the beguiling, undisciplined world of the late Gothic International Style painters, but *real* space in the sense that it functioned according to the immutable laws of God" (p. 30).

7. René Descartes, *Discourse on Method*, trans. John Veitch (La Salle, Ill.: Open Court, 1949), p. 21.

8. Pierre Simon, marquis de Laplace, *Introduction à la théorie analytique des probabilités*, in *Oeuvres complètes* (Paris, 1886), p. VI, translated and quoted in Mileč Čapec, *Philosophical Impact of Contemporary Physics* (New York: Van Nostrand, 1961), p. 122.

9. Gombrich, *Art and Illusion,* p. 5.

10. Joseph Conrad, *Heart of Darkness*, in *Heart of Darkness and The Secret Sharer* (New York: New American Library, 1950),p. 68. Subsequent page references will appear in the text.

11. William Faulkner, *Absalom, Absalom!* (New York: Random House, 1951), p. 8. Subsequent page references will appear in the text.

CHAPTER SIX

1. See my "Limits of Realism."

2. Robert Hughes, *Vladimir Nabokov*, National Education Television Film, 1966.

3. The concept of diabolic comedy has developed from my thinking since the publication of my *Stages of the Clown*. The germ of this essay will be found in chapter 6.

4. E. K. Chambers, *The Mediaeval Stage* (Oxford: Oxford University Press, 1903), p. 294.

5. T. McAlindon, "Comedy and Terror in Middle English Literature: The Diabolical Game," *Modern Language Review* 40 (July 1965): 321–32.

6. Enid Welsford, *The Fool: His Social and Literary History* (London: Faber & Faber, 1935), p. 231. Also see Barbara Swain, *Fools and Folly during the Middle Ages and the Renaissance* (New York: Columbia University Press, 1952), chap. 6.

7. Vladimir Nabokov, *Ada* (New York: McGraw-Hill, 1969), pp. 183–84.

8. "An Interview with Alain Robbe-Grillet, conducted by David Hayman," *Contemporary Literature* 16 (Summer 1975): 276.

9. Vladimir Nabokov, *Lolita* (New York: Berkley, 1966), p. 283. Subsequent page references will appear in the text.

10. "Lolita Lepidoptera," *New World Writing* 16 (1960): 58–84.

11. "*Lolita*: The Springboard of Parody," *Wisconsin Studies in Contemporary Literature* 8 (Spring 1967): 204–41; also in *Nabokov: The Man and His Work,* ed. L. S. Dembo (Madison: University of Wisconsin Press, 1967), pp. 106–43.

12. John Hollander, "The Perilous Magic of Nymphets," in *On Contemporary American Literature*, ed. Richard Kostelanetz (New York: Avon, 1964), pp. 477–80.

13. *Nikolai Gogol* (Norfolk, Conn.: New Directions, 1944), p. 144.

14. Ibid., p. 142.

15. Vladimir Nabokov, *Pale Fire* (New York: Berkley, 1968). Subsequent page references will appear in the text.

CHAPTER SEVEN

1. Thomas Pynchon, *Gravity's Rainbow* (New York: Viking, 1973), pp. 3, 1. Subsequent page references will appear in the text.

2. F. Scott Fitzgerald, *The Great Gatsby* (New York: Charles Scribner's Sons, 1925), p. 182.

3. Nathanael West, *The Day of the Locust*, in *Miss Lonelyhearts and The Day of the Locust* (New York: New Directions, 1950), p. 61.

4. Thomas Pynchon, *V.* (New York: Bantam, 1964), p. 8. Subsequent page references will appear in the text.

5. Quoted in Lewis Jacobs, *The Rise of the American Film: A Critical History* (New York: Teachers College Press, Columbia University, 1968), p. 189.

6. Thomas Pynchon, *The Crying of Lot 49* (New York: Bantam, 1967), p. 93. Subsequent page references will appear in the text.

7. Anne Mangel, "Maxwell's Demon, Entropy, Information: *The Crying of Lot 49*," *TriQuarterly* 20 (Winter 1971): 194-208.

8. Scott Simon, "A Character Index: *Gravity's Rainbow*," *Critique* 16 (December 1974): 68-72.

9. Scott Simon makes this point convincingly in "*Gravity's Rainbow* Described," *Critique* 16 (December 1974): 54-67.

CHAPTER EIGHT

1. Robert Coover, *The Public Burning* (New York: Viking, 1977), p. 4. Subsequent page references will appear in the text.

2. (New York: Putnam, 1966). Page references will appear in the text.

3. (New York: Random House, 1968; repr. New American Library, 1971). Page references will appear in the text.

4. (New York: E. P. Dutton, 1969; repr. New American Library, 1970). Page references will appear in the text.

5. "Surfiction—Four Propositions in Form of an Introduction," in *Surfiction: Fiction Now . . . and Tomorrow*, ed. Raymond Federman (Chicago: Swallow), pp. 5-15.

CHAPTER NINE

1. "Surfiction—Four Propositions in Form of an Introduction," pp. 7-8. I use the term "surfiction" rather than "metafiction" because it is more than fiction about itself, to emphasize both the flatness of its surface and the dynamic of its surf.

2. (New York: Fiction Collective, 1976). Pages are unnumbered.

3. Charles Caramello rightly insists that there is another dimension in Federman's fiction that derives from what cannot be said and what Federman refers to as "the central primal loss (X-X-X-X)." This is the experience of the holocaust, and particularly the extermination of Federman's family at Auschwitz. There is indeed an "edginess . . . that subtends" Federman's play, but less so in *Take It or Leave It* than in his next work, *The Voice in the Closet*, which has only been published in parts. See Caramello's "Flushing Out *The Voice in the Closet*," *SubStance* 20 (1978): 101-13.

4. (New York: New Directions, 1974), p. 1. Subsequent page references will appear in the text.

5. Developed from a point made by Kenneth Baker in his illuminating essay "Restricted Fiction: The Writing of Walter Abish," *New Directions in Prose and Poetry 35*, ed. J. Laughlin (New York: New Directions, 1977), p. 50.

6. "Death of the Novel" in *The Death of the Novel and Other Stories* (New York: Dial, 1969); *Up* (New York: Dell, 1968); *Out* (Chicago: Swallow, 1973); *98.6* (New York: Fiction Collective, 1975). Page references will appear in the text.

7. See Hawthorne's "Ethan Brand," from which I plagiarized this passage.

8. *Surfiction: Fiction Now and Tomorrow*, p. 7.

9. "Death of the Novel," p. 41.

10. See my "The Walker: Modern American Hero," *Massachusetts Review* 5 (Summer, 1964): 761-64, which uses Thoreau's "Walking" to define the American hero of the 1950s.

CHAPTER TEN

1. "Spatial Form in Modern Literature," *Sewanee Review* 53 (Spring, Summer, and Fall 1945): 221-40, 443-56, 643-53; reprinted in Joseph Frank, *The Widening Gyre: Crisis and Mastery in Modern Fiction* (New Brunswick, N.J.: Rutgers University Press, 1963), pp. 3-62.

2. *Space, Time, and Structure in the Modern Novel* (New York: New York University Press, 1971).

3. "Spatial Form," p. 15.

4. Trans. Paul de Man (New York: W. W. Norton, 1965), p. 107.

5. Eisenstein was also influenced by the ideograph: see "The Cinematographic Principle and the Ideogram" in *Film Form*. Eisenstein also misrepresented the effect of montage in his argument with Kuleshov and Pudovkin. He argues that the key to montage is not linking but collision, ignoring the fact that (except for montage within the shot, collisions of lines, volumes, etc.) montage is successive, the power and meaning being generated by the unique sequence.

6. Eisenstein, "Dickens, Griffith, and the Film Today," pp. 218, 224.

7. Virginia Woolf, *Mrs. Dalloway* (New York: Harcourt, Brace & World, 1953), p. 3. Subsequent citations are from pp. 3-24.

8. "Modern Fiction," in *The Common Reader*, First Series (New York: Harcourt, Brace & World, 1953), p. 154.

9. *Play,* in *Cascando and Other Short Dramatic Pieces* (New York: Grove Press, 1968), p. 45.

10. *Creative Evolution*, trans. Arthur Mitchell (New York: Random House, 1944), p. 7.

11. After the London production, Beckett suggested that the order of "interrogation" be varied in the second part. According to Ruby Cohn, "This radical change is in harmony with the play's timeless setting. Chronology was vitally important in earthly affairs, but chronology is already transcended in the replay of what was 'just play.' There can be no earthly reason to insist upon it or upon any temporal order. The speeches come to us in time, but it does not matter what time" (*Back to Beckett* [Princeton, N. J.: Princeton University Press, 1973], p. 200). Although this change is in harmony with the timeless setting, it also accentuates the temporal movement that the audience experiences. A practical dramatist involved in his productions, Beckett may have added this change to sustain the audience's interest—which is an interest in what happens next.

12. Jorge Luis Borges, "Pierre Menard, Author of *Don Quixote*," trans. Anthony Bonner, in *Ficciones* (London: Weidenfeld & Nicolson, 1962), pp. 54–55.

13. *The Philosophical Impact of Contemporary Physics* (New York: Van Nostrand, 1961), pp. 276 ff.

14. Gérard Genette calls the story's time "actual time" and the narrative order of events "pseudo-time." In doing so he betrays a bias for traditional, mimetic fiction, despite his great sensitivity to Proust. See his *Narrative Discourse: An Essay in Method*, trans. Jane Lewin (Ithaca, N. Y.: Cornell University Press, 1980).

15. Čapec, pp. 371–72.

Index

Abish, Walter, 118, 121–23, 131, 143. *See also Alphabetical Africa*

Absalom, Absalom!, 26, 36–37, 61, 63

Act without Words I, 51

Ada, 69

Adams, Henry, 36, 125, 141

After Many Years, 8

Alberti, Leon Battista, 58, 59, 60

Alphabetical Africa, 121–23

Alter, Robert, 7

Altman, Robert, 106–7

American Tragedy, An, 71, 84, 111

Appel, Alfred, Jr., 73

Arnheim, Rudolph, 6

Art and Illusion, 62

As I Lay Dying, 30

Assommoir, L', 12, 13

"Babysitter, The," 115–17, 118

"Bartleby the Scrivener," 111

Beckett, Samuel, 48–55, 65, 68, 119, 120, 139–40, 142–43. *See also Act without Words I; Happy Days; Krapp's Last Tape; Malone Dies; Molloy; Not I; Unnamable, The; Watt*

Bellow, Saul, 84

Bergson, Henri, 140

Black hole, 76, 82

Boccaccio, Giovanni, 59

Borges, Jorge Luis, 140

Budgen, Frank, 38, 43

Butler, Diana, 72–73

Čapec, Mileč, 141

Chaucer, Geoffrey, 59

Church, Margaret, 22

Conrad, Joseph, 15, 61, 62, 135–36. *See also Heart of Darkness; Nigger of the Narcissus, The*

Coover, Robert, 102–17, 118, 143. *See also* individual works

Crane, Hart, 84

Cross-cutting, 7, 8, 14, 90–91, 105, 108, 133

Crying of Lot 49, The, 91–96

Cubism, 25, 57

Dante, Alighieri, 72

Day of the Locust, The, 85–87, 101

Death of a Salesman, 111

Defoe, Daniel, 3, 5, 59

Descartes, René, 57, 59, 60, 65

Dialogue of the New Sciences, A, 58

Dickens, Charles, 7, 9, 133, 135

Discourse on Method, A, 59

Disney, Walt, 24, 25, 37

Dos Passos, John, 84, 125

Dostoyevsky, Fyodor, 76, 132

Dreiser, Theodore, 71, 84, 111. *See also American Tragedy, An*

Eisenstein, Sergei, 7, 9, 25, 42–47, 67, 133, 135

Expedition of Humphry Clinker, The, 6

Eye movement, 7, 14, 15, 16–23

Faulkner, William, 24–37, 39, 61, 63, 68, 84, 125, 131, 136. *See also Absalom, Absalom!; Flags in the Dust; Go Down, Moses; Light in August; Pylon; Reivers, The; Sanctuary*
Feast of fools, 68
Federman, 117, 118, 119–21, 131, 143
Fielding, Henry, 3, 4, 5, 59
Finnegans Wake, 55
Fitzgerald, F. Scott, 85, 125. *See also Great Gatsby, The*
Flags in the Dust, 25
Flaubert, Gustave, 11, 13, 133–34

Galileo Galilei, 58, 59, 60
Gance, Abel, 9
Gibson, James J., 145
Go Down, Moses, 26, 37
Gogol, Nikolai Vasilievich, 74
Gombrich, E. H., 62
Gravity's Rainbow, 84, 85, 96–101
Great Gatsby, The, 85–87, 101
Great Train Robbery, The, 8
Griffith, D. W., 7, 8, 25, 90, 91, 133, 135

Happy Days, 51, 120
Hawthorne, Nathaniel, 123
Hayman, David, 40
Heart of Darkness, The, 61, 62
Hemingway, Ernest, 125
Henderson the Rain King, 84
Huckleberry Finn, 125

Ingarden, Roman, 5
Intercutting. *See* Cross-cutting

James, Henry, 61
Jazz, 25
Jealousy, 118
Joseph Andrews, 3
Joyce, James, 16, 38–47, 67, 132, 136, 142. *See also* individual works

Kenner, Hugh, 57, 65
Kerouac, Jack, 125
Krapp's Last Tape, 51, 120

Laplace, Pierre Simon de, 60, 67
Light in August, 24, 25, 26, 31
Litz, A. Walton, 43
Lolita, 71–77, 82
Lonedale Operator, The, 8
Lonely Villa, The, 8
Long Day's Journey into Night, 84–85

Madame Bovary, 11, 13, 133–34
Mailer, Norman, 84
Malone Dies, 52–53, 120
Marx, Sam, 36
Melville, Herman, 72, 76, 111, 123, 125
Mickey Mouse, 24, 36
Miller, Arthur, 111
Miracle plays, 68
Moby-Dick, 72, 125
Moll Flanders, 3, 5
Molloy, 50–55, 120
Montage, 42–47, 64
Mrs. Dalloway, 136–139

Nabokov, Vladimir, 66–82, 143. *See also Ada; Lolita; Pale Fire*
Napoleon, 9
Narrator's view, 56–65
Narrator, hovering, 29–31, 64
Nigger of the Narcissus, The, 15, 136
98.6, 124, 127–30
Not I, 20
"Novel in motion" defined, 7

O'Neill, Eugene, 84–85
Oliver Twist, 9
On the Road, 125
Origin of the Brunists, The, 107–10, 114
Ortega y Gasset, 58
Out, 124, 125–27, 129

Pale Fire, 77–82
Pamela, 3, 5
Panofsky, Erwin, 24
Parmenides, 66
Paterson, 84
Pictures in motion, 9, 25–37

Pictures of motion, 9, 25
Picturing: traditional, phenomenal, modernist, 22–23
Play, 120, 139–40, 142
Porter, Edwin, 8
Portrait of the Artist as a Young Man, A, 16, 38, 67
Potemkin, 9, 57
Pound, Ezra, 132, 134, 141
Pricksongs and Descants, 115–17
Prometheus, 54
Public Burning, The, 102–7, 117
Pylon, 26, 131
Pynchon, Thomas, 36, 83–101, 143. *See also* individual works

Quantum Jump, 99

Rabelais, 119
Realism, 14
Reivers, The, 37
Richardson, Samuel, 3, 5, 59
Robbe-Grillet, Alain, 118, 119
Robinson Crusoe, 3, 5
Roman saturnalia, 68

Sanctuary, 24, 36
Sister Carrie, 71
Smollett, Tobias George, 6
Snyder, Joel, 145
Song of Myself, 84, 85, 87, 125
Sotie drama, 69
Sound and the Fury, The, 24, 28–29, 30, 136
Space: full and empty, 66–67
Spatial form, 132–43

Spencer, Sharon, 132
Spiegel, Alan, 11
Sterne, Laurence, 5, 59
Sukenick, Ronald, 118, 123–30, 131, 143. *See also 98.6; Out; Up*
Surfiction, 117, 119–30, 131
Sypher, Wylie, 147

Take It or Leave It, 119–21
Thoreau, Henry David, 125
Tom Jones, 4, 5
Tristram Shandy, 5
Turn of the Screw, The, 61
Twain, Mark, 125

U. S. A., 84
Ulysses, 38–47, 54, 67, 142
Universal Baseball Assoc., Inc., J. Henry Waugh, Prop., 110–15
Unnamable, The, 52–54, 65, 120
Unpicturable, 57
Up, 124–25

V., 87–91
Vertov, Dziga, 9

Watt, 48–51
West, Nathaniel, 85–87
Whitman, Walt, 83, 125
Why Are We in Vietnam?, 84
Williams, William Carlos, 84
Wolfe, Thomas, 84
Woolf, Virginia, 132, 136–39

Zeno, 66
Zola, Emile, 12, 13